the greatest evil is war

the greatest evil is war

CHRIS HEDGES

Seven Stories Press
NEW YORK • OAKLAND • LONDON

Seven Stories Press
140 Watts Street
New York, NY 10013
www.sevenstories.com

Library of Congress Cataloging-in-Publication Data

Names: Hedges, Chris, author.
Title: The greatest evil is war / Chris Hedges.
Description: New York : Seven Stories Press, [2022] | Includes
    bibliographical references and index.
Identifiers: LCCN 2022022165 | ISBN 9781644212936 (hardcover) | ISBN
    9781644212943 (ebook)
Subjects: LCSH: War--Moral and ethical aspects. | War (Philosophy)
Classification: LCC JZ6392 .H43 2022 | DDC 172/.42--dc23/eng/20220707
LC record available at https://lccn.loc.gov/2022022165

Permission to reprint Tomas Young's letter to Bush and Cheney,
courtesy of Claudia Young.

Permission to reprint excerpts from Jessica Goodell's *Shade It Black:
Death and After in Iraq*, courtesy of Casemate Publishers.

Brian Turner, "Ashbah" from *Here, Bullet*. Copyright © 2005 by Brian Turner.
Reprinted with the permission of The Permissions Company, LLC
on behalf of Alice James Books, www.alicejamesbooks.org.

College professors and high school and middle school teachers may order free
examination copies of Seven Stories Press titles. Visit https://www.sevenstories.com/
pg/resources-academics or email academics@sevenstories.com.

Printed in the USA.

9 8 7 6 5 4 3 2 1

For Kurt Schork and Miguel Gil Moreno de Mora,
killed on May 24, 2000, in an ambush in Sierra Leone.

Everything created by violence is senseless and useless.
It exists without a future; it will leave no trace.[1]

—VASILY GROSSMAN

CONTENTS

I.

The Greatest Evil Is War

Preemptive war, whether in Iraq or Ukraine, is a war crime. It does not matter if the war is launched on the basis of lies and fabrications, as was the case in Iraq, or because of the breaking of a series of agreements with Russia, including the promise by Washington not to extend NATO beyond the borders of a unified Germany, not to deploy thousands of NATO troops in Central and Eastern Europe, and not to meddle in the internal affairs of nations on Russia's border, as well as the refusal to implement the Minsk peace agreement. The invasion of Ukraine would, I expect, never have happened if these promises had been kept. Russia has every right to feel threatened, betrayed, and angry. But to understand is not to condone. The invasion of Ukraine, under post-Nuremberg laws, is a criminal war of aggression.

I know the instrument of war. War is not politics by other means. It is demonic. I spent two decades as a war correspondent in Central America, the Middle East, Africa, and the Balkans, where I covered the wars in Bosnia and Kosovo. I carry within me the ghosts of dozens of those swallowed up in the violence, including my close friend, Reuters correspondent

Kurt Schork, who was killed in an ambush in Sierra Leone with another friend, Miguel Gil Moreno de Mora.

I know the chaos and disorientation of war, the constant uncertainty and confusion. In a firefight you are only aware of what is happening a few feet around you. You desperately, and not always successfully, struggle to figure out where the firing is coming from to avoid being hit.

I have felt the helplessness and paralyzing fear which, years later, descend on me like a freight train in the middle of the night, leaving me wrapped in coils of terror, my heart racing, my body dripping with sweat.

I have heard the wails of those convulsed by grief as they clutch the bodies of friends and family, including children. I hear them still. It does not matter the language. Spanish. Arabic. Hebrew. Dinka. Serbo-Croatian. Albanian. Ukrainian. Russian. Death cuts through the linguistic barriers.

I know what wounds look like. Legs blown off. Heads imploded into a bloody, pulpy mass. Gaping holes in stomachs. Pools of blood. Cries of the dying, sometimes for their mothers. And the smell. The smell of death. The supreme sacrifice made for flies and maggots.

I was beaten by Iraqi and Saudi secret police. I was taken prisoner by the Contras in Nicaragua, who radioed back to their base in Honduras to see if they should kill me, and again in Basra after the first Gulf War in Iraq, never knowing if I would be executed, under constant guard and often without food, drinking out of mud puddles.

The primary lesson in war is that we as distinct individuals do not matter. We become numbers. Fodder. Objects. Life, once precious and sacred, becomes meaningless, sacrificed to the insatiable appetite of Mars. No one in wartime is exempt.

"We were expendable," Eugene Sledge wrote of his experiences as a Marine in the South Pacific in World War II. "It was difficult to accept. We come from a nation and a culture that values life and the individual. To find oneself in a situation where your life seems of little value is the ultimate in loneliness. It is a humbling experience."[2]

Sledge recalls a young Marine officer who had "one ghoulish, obscene tendency" of urinating into the mouths of Japanese corpses.[3]

The landscape of war is hallucinogenic. Sledge calls it "the kaleidoscope of the unreal."[4] It defies comprehension. War, like the Holocaust, as Barbara Foley wrote, is "unknowable." "Its full dimensions are inaccessible to the ideological framework that we have inherited from the liberal era."[5]

You have no concept of time in a firefight. A few minutes. A few hours. War, in an instant, obliterates homes and communities, all that was once familiar, and leaves behind smoldering ruins and a trauma that you carry for the rest of your life. I have tasted enough of war, enough of my own fear, my body turned to jelly, to know that war is always evil, the purest expression of death, dressed up in patriotic cant about liberty and democracy and sold to the naïve as a ticket to glory, honor, and courage. It is a toxic and seductive elixir. Those who survive, as Kurt Vonnegut wrote, struggle afterwards to "reinvent themselves and their universe," which, on some level, will never make sense again.

Walt Whitman, who tended wounded soldiers in hospitals during the Civil War, wrote in a heading in his notebook: "The real war will never get in the books."

"Its interior history will not only never be written," Whitman argues, "its practicality, minutiae of deeds and passions, will never be even suggested."[6]

War destroys all systems that sustain and nurture life—familial, economic, cultural, political, environmental, and social. Once war begins, no one, even those nominally in charge of waging war, knows what will happen, how the war will develop, how it can drive armies and nations towards suicidal folly. There are no good wars. None. This includes World War II, which has been sanitized and mythologized to celebrate American heroism, purity, and goodness. If truth is the first casualty in war, ambiguity is the second. The bellicose rhetoric embraced and amplified by the American press, demonizing Vladimir Putin and elevating the Ukrainians to the status of demigods, demanding more robust military intervention along with the crippling sanctions designed to bring down Putin's government, is infantile and dangerous. That the inverse version of the conflict is true in the Russian media fuels the insanity.

There were no discussions about pacifism in the basements in Sarajevo when we were being hit with hundreds of Serbian shells a day and under constant sniper fire. It made sense to defend the city. It made sense to kill or be killed. The Bosnian Serb soldiers in the Drina Valley, Vukovar, and Srebrenica had amply demonstrated their capacity for murderous rampages, including the gunning down of hundreds of soldiers and civilians and the wholesale rape of women and girls. But this did not save any of the defenders in Sarajevo from the poison of violence, the soul-destroying force that is war. I knew a Bosnian soldier who heard a sound behind a door while patrolling on the outskirts of Sarajevo. He fired a burst from his AK-47 through the door. A delay of a few seconds in combat can mean death. When he opened the door, he found the bloody remains of a twelve-year-old girl. His daughter was twelve. He never recovered.

II.

Chronicle of a War Foretold

I was in Central and Eastern Europe in 1989, reporting on the revolutions that overthrew the ossified communist dictatorships that led to the collapse of the Soviet Union. It was a time of hope. NATO, with the breakup of the Soviet empire, became obsolete. President Mikhail Gorbachev reached out to Washington and Europe to build a new security pact that would include Russia, perhaps one that would lead to joining NATO. Secretary of State James Baker in the Reagan administration, along with West German Foreign Minister Hans-Dietrich Genscher, assured the Soviet leader that if Germany was unified NATO would not be extended beyond the new borders. The commitment not to expand NATO, also made by Great Britain and France, appeared to herald a new global order. We saw the peace dividend dangled before us, the promise that the massive expenditures on weapons that characterized the Cold War would be converted into expenditures on social programs and infrastructures that had long been neglected to feed the insatiable appetite of the military.

There was a near universal understanding among diplomats and political leaders at the time that any attempt to expand

NATO was foolish, an unwarranted provocation against Russia that would obliterate the ties and bonds that happily emerged at the end of the Cold War.

How naïve we were. The war industry did not intend to shrink its power or its profits. It set out almost immediately to recruit the former Communist Bloc countries into the European Union and NATO. Countries that joined NATO, which now include Poland, Hungary, the Czech Republic, Bulgaria, Estonia, Latvia, Lithuania, Romania, Slovakia, Slovenia, Albania, Croatia, Montenegro, and North Macedonia, were forced to reconfigure their militaries, often through hefty loans, to become compatible with NATO military hardware. The steady shipments of European and U.S. weapons into Ukraine were turning the country, despite Russian protests, into a de facto NATO member.

There would be no peace dividend. The expansion of NATO swiftly became a multibillion-dollar bonanza for the corporations that had profited from the Cold War. (Poland, for example, in a recent arms deal, will spend $6 billion on M1 Abrams tanks and other U.S. military equipment.) If Russia would not acquiesce to again being the enemy, then Russia would be pressured into becoming the enemy. And here we are. On the brink of another Cold War, one from which only the war industry will profit while, as W. H. Auden wrote, "the little children died in the streets."[7]

The consequences of pushing NATO up to the borders with Russia—there is now a NATO missile base in Poland one hundred miles from the Russian border—were well known to policy makers. Yet they did it anyway. It made no geopolitical sense. But it made commercial sense. War, after all, is a business, a very lucrative one. It is why we spent two decades in

Afghanistan although there was near universal consensus after a few years of fruitless fighting that we had waded into a quagmire we could never win.

In a classified diplomatic cable obtained and released by WikiLeaks dated February 1, 2008, written from Moscow and addressed to the Joint Chiefs of Staff, NATO–European Union Cooperative, National Security Council, Russia Moscow Political Collective, Secretary of Defense, and Secretary of State, there was an unequivocal understanding that expanding NATO risked an eventual conflict with Russia, especially over Ukraine. The cable reads:

> Not only does Russia perceive encirclement [by NATO], and efforts to undermine Russia's influence in the region, but it also fears unpredictable and uncontrolled consequences which would seriously affect Russian security interests. Experts tell us that Russia is particularly worried that the strong divisions in Ukraine over NATO membership, with much of the ethnic-Russian community against membership, could lead to a major split, involving violence or at worst, civil war. In that eventuality, Russia would have to decide whether to intervene; a decision Russia does not want to have to face. . . . Dmitri Trenin, Deputy Director of the Carnegie Moscow Center, expressed concern that Ukraine was, in the long-term, the most potentially destabilizing factor in U.S.-Russian relations, given the level of emotion and neuralgia triggered by its quest for NATO membership. . . . Because membership remained divisive in Ukrainian domestic politics, it created an opening for Russian intervention. Trenin

expressed concern that elements within the Russian establishment would be encouraged to meddle, stimulating U.S. overt encouragement of opposing political forces, and leaving the U.S. and Russia in a classic confrontational posture.[8]

The Obama administration, not wanting to further inflame tensions with Russia, blocked arms sales to Kyiv. But this act of prudence was abandoned by the Trump and Biden administrations. Weapons from the U.S. and Great Britain are pouring into Ukraine, part of the $1.5 billion in promised military aid. The equipment includes hundreds of sophisticated Javelins and NLAW anti-tank weapons, despite repeated protests by Moscow.

The United States and its NATO allies have no intention of sending troops to Ukraine. Rather, they will flood the country with weapons, which is what they did in the 2008 conflict between Russia and Georgia. Bog down Russian forces with Ukrainian corpses.

The conflict in Ukraine echoes the novel *Chronicle of a Death Foretold* by Gabriel García Márquez. In the novel it is acknowledged by the narrator that "there had never been a death more foretold"[9] and yet no one was able or willing to stop it. All of us who reported from Central and Eastern Europe in 1989 knew the consequences of provoking Russia, and yet few have raised their voices to halt the madness. The methodical steps towards war took on a life of their own, moving us like sleepwalkers towards disaster.

Once NATO expanded into Central and Eastern Europe, the Clinton administration promised Moscow that NATO combat troops would not be stationed there, the defining issue of the 1997 Founding Act on Mutual Relations, Cooperation and Security between NATO and the Russian Federation. This promise again turned out to be a lie. Then, in 2014, the U.S. helped oust Ukrainian President Viktor Yanukovych, who sought to build an economic alliance with Russia rather than the European Union. Of course, once integrated into the European Union, as seen in the rest of Central and Eastern Europe, the next step is integration into NATO. Russia, spooked by the 2014 U.S. intervention in Ukraine, alarmed at the overtures by the EU and NATO, then annexed Crimea, largely populated by Russian speakers. And the death spiral that led us to the conflict currently underway in Ukraine became unstoppable.

The war state needs enemies to sustain itself. When an enemy can't be found, an enemy is manufactured. Putin has become, in the words of Senator Angus King, the new Hitler, out to grab Ukraine and the rest of Central and Eastern Europe. The full-throated cries for war, echoed shamelessly by the press, are justified by draining the conflict of historical context, by elevating ourselves as the saviors and casting whomever we oppose, from Saddam Hussein to Putin, as the new Nazi leader.

III.

Worthy and Unworthy Victims

Rulers divide the world into worthy and unworthy victims, those we are allowed to pity, such as Ukrainians enduring the hell of modern warfare, and those whose suffering is minimized, dismissed, or ignored. The terror we and our allies carry out against Iraqi, Palestinian, Syrian, Libyan, Somali, and Yemeni civilians is part of the regrettable cost of war. We, echoing the empty promises from Moscow, claim we do not target civilians. Rulers always paint their militaries as humane, there to serve and protect. Collateral damage happens, but it is regrettable.

This lie can only be sustained among those who are unfamiliar with the explosive ordnance and large kill zones of missiles; iron fragmentation bombs; mortar, artillery, and tank shells; and belt-fed machine guns. This bifurcation into worthy and unworthy victims, as Edward Herman and Noam Chomsky point out in *Manufacturing Consent: The Political Economy of the Mass Media*, is a key component of propaganda, especially in war. The Russian-speaking population in Ukraine, to Moscow, are worthy victims. Russia is their savior. The millions of Ukrainian families cowering in basements and subways, or forced to flee Ukraine, are unworthy victims. Ukrainian fighters are condemned as "Nazis."

Worthy victims allow citizens to see themselves as empathetic, compassionate, and just. Worthy victims are an effective tool to demonize the aggressor. They are used to obliterate nuance and ambiguity. Mention the provocations carried out by the Western alliance and you are dismissed as a Putin apologist. It is to taint the sainthood of the worthy victims, and by extension ourselves.

We are good. They are evil. Worthy victims are used not only to express sanctimonious outrage, but to stoke self-adulation and a poisonous nationalism. The cause becomes sacred, a religious crusade. Fact-based evidence is abandoned, as it was during the calls to invade Iraq. Charlatans, liars, con artists, fake defectors, and opportunists become experts, used to fuel the conflict.

Celebrities, who, like the powerful, carefully orchestrate their public image, pour out their hearts to worthy victims. Hollywood stars such as George Clooney made trips to Darfur to denounce the war crimes being committed by Khartoum at the same time the U.S. was killing scores of civilians in Iraq and Afghanistan. The war in Iraq was as savage as the slaughter in Darfur, but to express outrage at what was happening to unworthy victims was to become branded as the enemy.

Saddam Hussein's attacks on the Kurds after the first Gulf War were considered worthy victims, while Israeli persecution of the Palestinians, subjected to relentless bombing campaigns by the Israeli air force, artillery and tank units, with hundreds of dead and wounded, were a footnote. At the height of Stalin's purges in the 1930s, worthy victims were the Republicans battling the fascists in the Spanish civil war. Soviet citizens were mobilized to send aid and assistance. Unworthy victims were the millions of people Stalin sent to the gulags, sometimes after tawdry show trials, and executed.

While I was reporting from El Salvador in 1984, the Catholic priest Jerzy Popiełuszko was murdered by the regime in Poland. His death was used to excoriate the Polish communist government, a stark contrast to the response of the Reagan administration to the rape and murder of four Catholic missionaries in 1980 in El Salvador by the Salvadoran National Guard. President Ronald Reagan's administration sought to blame the three nuns and a lay worker for their own deaths. Jeane Kirkpatrick, Reagan's ambassador to the United Nations, said, "The nuns were not just nuns. The nuns were also political activists." Secretary of State Alexander Haig speculated that "perhaps they ran a roadblock."[10]

For the Reagan administration, the murdered churchwomen were unworthy victims. The right-wing government in El Salvador, armed and backed by the United States, joked at the time, *Haz patria, mata un cura* (Be a patriot, kill a priest). Archbishop Óscar Romero had been assassinated in March of 1980. Nine years later, the Salvadoran regime would gun down six Jesuits and two others at their residence on the campus of Central American University in San Salvador. Between 1977 and 1989, death squads and soldiers killed thirteen priests in El Salvador.

It is not that worthy victims do not suffer, nor that they are not deserving of our support and compassion; it is that worthy victims alone are rendered human, people like us, and unworthy victims are not. It helps, of course, when, as in Ukraine, they are white. But the missionaries murdered in El Salvador were also white and American, and yet it was not enough to shake U.S. support for the country's military dictatorship.

"The mass media never explain why Andrei Sakharov is worthy and José Luis Massera, in Uruguay, is unworthy," Herman and Chomsky write. They continue:

> The attention and general dichotomization occur "naturally" as a result of the working of the filters, but the result is the same as if a commissar had instructed the media: "Concentrate on the victims of enemy powers and forget about the victims of friends." Reports of the abuses of worthy victims not only pass through the filters; they may also become the basis of sustained propaganda campaigns. If the government or corporate community and the media feel that a story is useful as well as dramatic, they focus on it intensively and use it to enlighten the public.

This was true, for example, of the shooting down by the Soviets of the Korean Air Lines flight 007 in early September 1983, which permitted an extended campaign of denigration of an official enemy and greatly advanced Reagan administration arms plans. As Bernard Gwertzman noted complacently in the *New York Times* of August 31, 1984, U.S. officials "assert that worldwide criticism of the Soviet handling of the crisis has strengthened the United States in its relations with Moscow." In sharp contrast, the shooting down by Israel of a Libyan civilian airliner in February 1973 led to no outcry in the West, no denunciations for "cold-blooded murder," and no boycott. This difference in treatment was explained by the *New York Times* precisely on the grounds of utility in a 1973 editorial: "No useful purpose is served by an acrimonious debate over the assignment of blame for the downing of a Libyan airliner in the Sinai Peninsula last week." There was a very "useful purpose" served by focusing on the Soviet act, and a massive propaganda campaign ensued.[11]

It is impossible to hold those responsible for war crimes accountable if worthy victims are deserving of justice and unworthy victims are not. If Russia should be crippled with sanctions for invading Ukraine, which I believe it should, the United States should have been crippled with sanctions for invading Iraq, a war launched based on lies and fabricated evidence.

Imagine if America's largest banks, JPMorgan Chase, Citibank, Bank of America, and Wells Fargo, were cut off from the international banking system. Imagine if our oligarchs, Jeff Bezos, Jamie Dimon, Bill Gates, and Elon Musk, as venal as Russian oligarchs, had their assets frozen and estates and luxury yachts seized. (Bezos's yacht is the largest in the world, cost an estimated $500 million, and is about fifty-seven feet longer than a football field.) Imagine if leading political figures, such as George W. Bush and Dick Cheney, and U.S. "oligarchs" were blocked from traveling under visa restrictions. Imagine if the world's biggest shipping lines suspended shipments to and from the United States. Imagine if U.S. international media news outlets were forced off the air. Imagine if we were blocked from purchasing spare parts for our commercial airlines, and our passenger jets were banned from European air space. Imagine if our athletes were barred from hosting or participating in international sporting events. Imagine if our symphony conductors and opera stars were forbidden from performing unless they denounced the Iraq war and, in a kind of perverted loyalty oath, condemned George W. Bush.

The rank hypocrisy is stunning. Some of the same officials that orchestrated the invasion of Iraq, who under international law are war criminals for carrying out a preemptive war, are now chastising Russia for its violation of international law. The U.S. bombing campaign of Iraqi urban centers, called "Shock and Awe," saw the dropping of 3,000 bombs on civilian areas that killed more than 7,000 noncombatants in the first two months of the war.

"I have argued that when you invade a sovereign nation, that is a war crime," Harris Faulkner, a Fox News host said (with a straight face) to Condoleezza Rice, who served as Bush's national security adviser during the Iraq War.

"It is certainly against every principle of international law and international order, and that is why throwing the book at them now in terms of economic sanctions and punishments is also a part of it," Rice said. "And I think the world is there. Certainly, NATO is there. He's managed to unite NATO in ways that I didn't think I would ever see after the end of the Cold War."

Rice inadvertently made a case for why she should be put on trial with the rest of Bush's enablers. She famously justified the invasion of Iraq by stating: "The problem here is that there will always be some uncertainty about how quickly he can acquire nuclear weapons. But we don't want the smoking gun to be a mushroom cloud." Her rationale for preemptive war, which under post-Nuremberg laws is a criminal war of aggression, is no different than that peddled by Russian Foreign Minister Sergey Lavrov, who says the Russia invasion is being carried out to prevent Ukraine from obtaining nuclear weapons.

Only rarely is this hypocrisy exposed as when U.S. Ambassador to the United Nations Linda Thomas-Greenfield told the

body: "We've seen videos of Russian forces moving exception-
ally lethal weaponry into Ukraine, which has no place on the
battlefield. That includes cluster munitions and vacuum bombs
which are banned under the Geneva Convention." Hours later,
the official transcript of her remark was amended to tack on
the words "*if they are directed against civilians.*" This is because
the U.S., which like Russia never ratified the Convention on
Cluster Munitions treaty, regularly uses cluster munitions. It
used them in Vietnam, Laos, Cambodia, and Iraq. It has provided them to Saudi Arabia for use in Yemen. Russia has yet to
come close to the tally of civilian deaths from cluster munitions
delivered by the U.S. military.

And this brings me to RT America, where I had a show
called *On Contact*. RT America is now off the air after being
deplatformed and unable to disseminate its content. This was
long the plan of the U.S. government. The invasion of Ukraine
gave Washington the opening to shut RT down. The network
had a tiny media footprint. But it gave a platform to American
dissidents who challenged corporate capitalism, imperialism,
war, and the American oligarchy.

My public denunciation of the invasion of Ukraine was
treated very differently by RT America than my public denunciation of the Iraq war was treated by my former employer, the
New York Times. RT America made no comment, publicly or
privately, about my condemnation of the invasion of Ukraine
in my ScheerPost column. Nor did RT comment about
statements by Jesse Ventura, a Vietnam veteran and former
Minnesota governor, who also had a show on RT America, and
who wrote: "20 years ago, I lost my job because I opposed the
Iraq War and the invasion of Iraq. Today, I still stand for peace.
As I've said previously, I oppose this war, this invasion, and

if standing up for peace costs me another job, so be it. I will always speak out against war."

RT America was shut down six days after I denounced the invasion of Ukraine. If the network had continued, Ventura and I might have paid with our jobs, but at least for those six days they kept us on air.

The *New York Times* issued a formal written reprimand in 2003 that forbade me to speak about the war in Iraq, although I had been the newspaper's Middle East Bureau Chief, had spent seven years in the Middle East, and was an Arabic speaker. This reprimand set me up to be fired. If I violated the prohibition, under guild rules, the paper had grounds to terminate my employment. John Burns, another foreign correspondent at the paper, publicly supported the invasion of Iraq. He did not receive a reprimand.

My repeated warnings in public forums about the chaos and bloodbath the invasion of Iraq would trigger, which turned out to be correct, was not an opinion. It was an analysis based on years of experience in the region, including in Iraq, and an intimate understanding of the instrument of war those in the Bush White House lacked. But it challenged the dominant narrative and was silenced. This same censorship of anti-war sentiment is happening now in Russia, but we should remember it happened here during the inception and initial stages of the invasion of Iraq.

Those of us who opposed the Iraq war, no matter how much experience we had in the region, were marginalized and vilified. Ventura, who had a three-year contract with MSNBC, saw his show canceled.

Those who were cheerleaders for the war, such as George Packer, Thomas Friedman, Paul Berman, Michael Ignatieff,

Leon Wieseltier, and Nick Kristof, a group Tony Judt called "Bush's useful idiots," dominated the media landscape. They painted the Iraqis as oppressed, worthy victims, whom the U.S. military would set free. The plight of women under the Taliban was a rallying cry to bomb and occupy the country. These courtiers to power served the interests of the power elite and the war industry. They differentiated between worthy and unworthy victims. It was a good career move. And they knew it.

There was very little dispute about the folly of invading Iraq among reporters in the Middle East, but most did not want to jeopardize their positions by speaking publicly. They did not want my fate to become their own, especially after I was booed off a commencement stage in Rockford, Illinois, for delivering an anti-war speech and became a punching bag for right-wing media. I would walk through the newsroom and reporters I had known for years looked down or turned their heads as if I had leprosy. My career was finished. And not just at the *New York Times* but with any major media organization. This is where I was, orphaned, when Robert Scheer, who had lost his job as a columnist for the *Los Angeles Times* because of his opposition to the war, recruited me to write for the website Truthdig, which he then edited.

What Russia is doing militarily in Ukraine, at least up to now, was more than matched by our own savagery in Iraq, Afghanistan, Syria, Libya, and Vietnam. This is an inconvenient fact that the press, awash in moral posturing, will not address.

No one has mastered the art of technowar and wholesale slaughter like the U.S. military. When atrocities leak out, such as the massacre of more than five hundred unarmed villagers at My Lai in Vietnam or the torture of prisoners in Abu Ghraib, the press does its duty by branding them aberrations. The truth is that these killings and abuse are deliberate. They are orchestrated at the senior levels of the military. Infantry units, assisted by long-range artillery, fighter jets, heavy bombers, missiles, drones, and helicopters, level vast swaths of "enemy" territory, killing most of the inhabitants. The U.S. military, during the invasion of Iraq from Kuwait, created a six-mile-wide free-fire zone that killed hundreds if not thousands of Iraqis. The indiscriminate killing ignited the Iraqi insurgency.

When I entered southern Iraq in the first Gulf War, it was flattened. Villages and towns were smoldering ruins. Bodies of the dead, including women and children, lay scattered on the ground. Water purification systems had been bombed. Power stations had been bombed. Schools and hospitals had been bombed. Bridges had been bombed. The United States military always wages war by "overkill," which is why it dropped the equivalent of 640 Hiroshima-size atomic bombs on Vietnam, most actually falling on the south, where our purported Vietnamese allies resided. It unloaded in Vietnam more than 70 million tons of herbicidal agents, three million rockets tipped with white phosphorus—which will burn its way entirely through a body—and an estimated 400,000 tons of jellied incendiary napalm.[12]

"Thirty-five percent of the victims," Nick Turse wrote of the war in Vietnam, "died within 15 to 20 minutes." Death from the skies, like death on the ground, was often unleashed capriciously. "It was not out of the ordinary for US troops in Vietnam to blast a whole village or bombard a wide area in an effort to kill a single sniper."[13]

Vietnamese villagers, including women, children, and the elderly, were often herded into tiny barbed-wire enclosures known as "cow cages." They were subjected to electric shocks, gang-raped, and tortured by being hung upside down and beaten—a practice euphemistically called "the plane ride"—until unconscious. Fingernails were ripped out. Fingers were dismembered. Detainees were slashed with knives. They were beaten senseless with baseball bats and waterboarded. Targeted assassinations, orchestrated by CIA death squads, were ubiquitous.

Wholesale destruction, including of human beings, is orgiastic. The ability to unleash sheets of automatic rifle fire, hundreds of rounds of belt-fed machine-gun fire, 90-mm tank rounds, endless grenades, mortars, and artillery shells on a village, sometimes supplemented by gigantic 2,700-pound explosive projectiles fired from battleships along the coast, was a perverted form of entertainment in Vietnam, as it became later in the Middle East. U.S. troops litter the countryside with claymore mines. These are our calling cards: canisters of napalm, daisy-cutter bombs, anti-personnel rockets, high-explosive rockets, incendiary rockets, cluster bombs, high-explosive shells, and iron fragmentation bombs—including the 40,000-pound bomb loads dropped by giant B-52 Stratofortress bombers—along with chemical defoliants and chemical gases dropped from the sky. Vast areas are designated free-fire zones (a term later changed by the military to the more neutral-sounding "specified strike zone"), in which everyone is considered the enemy, even the elderly, women, and children.

Soldiers and Marines who attempt to report the war crimes they witness can face a fate worse than being pressured, discredited, or ignored. On Sepember 12, 1969, as Nick Turse wrote in his book *Kill Anything That Moves: The Real American War in Vietnam*, George Chunko sent a letter to his parents explaining how his unit had entered a home that had a young Vietnamese woman, four young children, an elderly man, and a military-age male inside. It appeared the younger man was AWOL from the South Vietnamese army. The young man was stripped naked and tied to a tree. His wife fell to her knees and begged the soldiers for mercy. The prisoner, Chunko wrote, was "ridiculed, slapped around and [had] mud rubbed into this face."[14] He was then executed.

A day after he wrote the letter, Chunko was killed. Chunko's parents, Turse wrote, "suspected that their son had been murdered to cover up the crime."[15]

All of this remains unspoken as we express our anguish for the people of Ukraine and revel in our moral superiority. The life of a Palestinian or an Iraqi child is as precious as the life of a Ukrainian child. No one should live in fear and terror. No one should be sacrificed on the altar of Mars. But until all victims are worthy, until all who wage war are held accountable and brought to justice, this hypocritical game of life and death will continue. Some human beings will be worthy of life. Others will not. Drag Putin off to the International Criminal Court and put him on trial. But make sure George W. Bush is in the cell next to him. If we can't see ourselves, we can't see anyone else. And this blindness leads to catastrophe.

IV.

The Pimps of War

The same cabal of warmongering pundits, foreign policy specialists, and government officials, year after year, debacle after debacle, smugly dodge responsibility for the military fiascos they orchestrate. They are protean, shifting adroitly with the political winds, moving from the Republican Party to the Democratic Party and then back again, mutating from cold warriors to neocons to liberal interventionists. Pseudo-intellectuals, they exude a cloying Ivy League snobbery as they sell perpetual fear, perpetual war, and a racist worldview, where the lesser breeds of the earth only understand violence.

They are pimps of war, puppets of the Pentagon, a state within a state, and the defense contractors who lavishly fund their think tanks—Project for the New American Century, American Enterprise Institute, Foreign Policy Initiative, Institute for the Study of War, Atlantic Council, and Brookings Institution. Like some mutant strain of an antibiotic-resistant bacteria, they cannot be vanquished. It does not matter how wrong they are, how absurd their theories, how many times they lie or denigrate other cultures and societies as uncivilized or how many murderous military interventions go bad. They are immovable props, the parasitic mandarins of power that are vomited up in the dying days of any empire, including ours, leaping from one self-defeating catastrophe to the next.

I reported on the suffering, misery, and murderous rampages these shills for war engineered and funded. My first encounter with them was in Central America. Elliott Abrams—convicted of providing misleading testimony to Congress on the Iran-Contra Affair and later pardoned by President George H. W. Bush so he could return to government to sell us the Iraq War— and Robert Kagan, director of the State Department's public diplomacy office for Latin America—were propagandists for the brutal military regimes in El Salvador and Guatemala, as well as the rapists and homicidal thugs that made up the rogue Contra forces fighting the Sandinista government in Nicaragua, which they illegally funded. Their job was to discredit our reporting.

They, and their coterie of fellow war lovers, went on to push for the expansion of NATO in Central and Eastern Europe after the fall of the Berlin Wall, violating an agreement not to extend NATO beyond the borders of a unified Germany and recklessly antagonizing Russia. They were and are cheerleaders for the apartheid state of Israel, justifying its war crimes against Palestinians and myopically conflating Israel's interests with our own. They advocated for air strikes in Serbia, calling for the U.S. to "take out" Slobodan Milošević. They were the authors of the policy to invade Afghanistan, Iraq, Syria and Libya. Robert Kagan and William Kristol, with their typical cluelessness, wrote in April 2002 that "the road that leads to real security and peace" is "the road that runs through Baghdad."[16]

We saw how that worked out. That road led to the dissolution of Iraq, the destruction of its civilian infrastructure, including the obliteration of eighteen of twenty electricity-generating plants and nearly all the water-pumping and sanitation systems during a forty-three-day period when 90,000 tons of bombs were rained down on the country, the rise of radical jihadist groups throughout the region, and failed states. The war in Iraq, along with the humiliating defeat in Afghanistan, shredded the illusion of U.S. military and global hegemony. It also inflicted on Iraqis, who had nothing to do with the attacks of 9/11, the widespread killing of civilians, the torture and sexual humiliation of Iraqi prisoners, and the ascendancy of Iran as the preeminent power in the region. They continue to call for a war with Iran, with Fred Kagan stating that "there is nothing we can do short of attacking to force Iran to give up its nuclear weapons." They pushed for the overthrow of President Nicolás Maduro, after trying to do the same to Hugo Chávez, in Venezuela. They have targeted Daniel Ortega, their old nemesis in Nicaragua.

They embrace a purblind nationalism that prohibits them from seeing the world from any perspective other than their own. They know nothing about the machinery of war, its consequences, or its inevitable blowback. They know nothing about the peoples and cultures they target for violent regeneration. They believe in their divine right to impose their "values" on others by force. Fiasco after fiasco. Now they are stoking a war with Russia.

"The nationalist is by definition an ignoramus," Yugoslav writer Danilo Kiš observed. "Nationalism is the line of least resistance, the easy way. The nationalist is untroubled, he knows or thinks he knows what his values are, his, that's to say national, that's to say the values of the nation he belongs to, ethical and political; he is not interested in others, they are no concern of his, hell—it's other people (other nations, another tribe). They don't even need investigating. The nationalist sees other people in his own image—as nationalists."[17]

The Biden administration is filled with these ignoramuses, including Joe Biden. Victoria Nuland, the wife of Robert Kagan, serves as Biden's undersecretary of state for political affairs. Antony Blinken is secretary of state. Jake Sullivan is national security advisor. They come from this cabal of moral and intellectual trolls that includes Kimberly Kagan, the wife of Fred Kagan, who founded the Institute for the Study of War, William Kristol, Max Boot, John Podhoretz, Gary Schmitt, Richard Perle, Douglas Feith, David Frum, and others. Many were once staunch Republicans or, like Nuland, served in Republican and Democratic administrations. Nuland was the principal deputy foreign policy adviser to Vice President Dick Cheney.

They are united by the demand for larger and larger defense budgets and an ever-expanding military. Julien Benda called these courtiers to power "the self-made barbarians of the intelligentsia."

"There will be no substitute for military strength, and we do not have enough," wrote Abrams in March 2022 for the Council on Foreign Relations, where he is a senior fellow: "It should be crystal clear now that a larger percentage of GDP will need to be spent on defense. We will need more conventional strength in ships and planes. We will need to match the Chinese in advanced military technology, but at the other end of the spectrum, we may need many more tanks if we have to station thousands in Europe, as we did during the Cold War. (The total number of American tanks permanently stationed in Europe today is zero.) Persistent efforts to diminish even further the size of our nuclear arsenal or prevent its modernization were always bad ideas, but now, as China and Russia are modernizing their nuclear weaponry and appear to have no interest in negotiating new limits, such restraints should be completely abandoned. Our nuclear arsenal will need to be modernized and expanded so that we will never face the kinds of threats Putin is now making from a position of real nuclear inferiority."[18]

They once railed against liberal weakness and appeasement. But they swiftly migrated to the Democratic Party rather than support Donald Trump, who showed no desire to start a conflict with Russia and who called the invasion of Iraq a "big, fat mistake." Besides, as they correctly pointed out, Hillary Clinton was a fellow neocon. And liberals wonder why nearly half the electorate, who revile these arrogant, unaccountable power brokers, as they should, voted for Trump.

These ideologues did not see the corpses of their victims. I did. Including children. Every dead body I stood over in Guatemala, El Salvador, Nicaragua, Gaza, Iraq, Sudan, Yemen or Kosovo, month after month, year after year, exposed their moral bankruptcy, their intellectual dishonesty, and their sick bloodlust. They did not serve in the military. Their children do not serve in the military. But they eagerly ship young American men and women off to fight and die for their self-delusional dreams of empire and American hegemony. Or, as in Ukraine, they provide hundreds of millions of dollars in weaponry and logistical support to sustain long and bloody proxy wars.

Historical time stopped for them with the end of World War II. The overthrow of democratically elected governments by the U.S. during the Cold War in Indonesia, Guatemala, the Congo, Iran, and Chile (where the CIA oversaw the assassination of the commander-in-chief of the army, General René Schneider, and President Salvador Allende), the Bay of Pigs, the atrocities and war crimes that defined the wars in Vietnam,

Cambodia, and Laos, even the disasters they manufactured in the Middle East, have disappeared into the black hole of their collective historical amnesia. American global domination, they claim, is benign, a force for good, "benevolent hegemony." The world, Charles Krauthammer insisted, welcomes "our power." All enemies, from Saddam Hussein to Vladimir Putin, are the new Hitler. All U.S. interventions are a fight for freedom that make the world a safer place. All refusals to bomb and occupy another country are a 1938 Munich moment, a pathetic retreat from confronting evil by the new Neville Chamberlain.

"America has not yet understood what the Second World War was like and has thus been unable to use such understanding to reinterpret and redefine the national reality and to arrive at something like public maturity," wrote Paul Fussell, who as a lieutenant led a rifle platoon in the 103rd Infantry Division in France and was severely wounded in the spring of 1945.[19]

We do have enemies abroad. But our most dangerous enemy is within.

The warmongers build a campaign against a country such as Iraq or Russia and then wait for a crisis—they call it the next Pearl Harbor—to justify the unjustifiable. In 1998, William Kristol and Robert Kagan, along with a dozen other prominent neoconservatives, wrote an open letter to President Bill Clinton denouncing his policy of containment of Iraq as a failure and demanding that he go to war to overthrow Saddam Hussein. To continue the "course of weakness and drift," they warned, was to "put our interests and our future at risk."

Huge majorities in Congress, Republican and Democrat, rushed to pass the Iraq Liberation Act. Few Democrats or Republicans dared be seen as soft on national security. The act stated that the United States government would work to "remove the regime headed by Saddam Hussein" and authorized $99 million towards that goal, some of it being used to fund Ahmed Chalabi's Iraqi National Congress that would become instrumental in disseminating the fabrications and lies used to justify the Iraq war during the administration of George W. Bush.

The attacks of 9/11 gave the war party its opening, first with Afghanistan, then Iraq. Krauthammer, who knew nothing about the Muslim world, wrote that "the way to tame the Arab street is not with appeasement and sweet sensitivity but with raw power and victory . . . The elementary truth that seems to elude the experts again and again . . . is that power is its own reward. Victory changes everything, psychologically above all. The psychology in the [Middle East] is now one of fear and deep respect for American power. Now is the time to use it."[20]

William Kristol, testifying before the Senate Foreign Relations Committee on February 7, 2002, laid out the case for a war with Iraq and the myriad of benefits the overthrow of Saddam Hussein would bring to the United States:

> The larger question with respect to Iraq, as with Afghanistan, is what happens after the combat is concluded. The Iraqi opposition lacks the military strength of the Afghan Northern Alliance; however, it claims a political legitimacy that might even be greater. And, as in Kabul but also as in the Kurdish and Shi'ite regions of Iraq in 1991, American and alliance forces will be welcomed in Baghdad as liberators. Indeed, reconstructing Iraq may prove to be a less difficult task than the challenge of building a viable state in Afghanistan.
>
> The political, strategic and moral rewards would also be even greater. A friendly, free, and oil-producing Iraq

would leave Iran isolated and Syria cowed; the Palestinians more willing to negotiate seriously with Israel; and Saudi Arabia with less leverage over policymakers here and in Europe. Removing Saddam Hussein and his henchmen from power presents a genuine opportunity—one President Bush sees clearly—to transform the political landscape of the Middle East.[21]

It did, of course, but not in ways that benefited the U.S.

They lust for apocalyptic global war. Fred Kagan, the brother of Robert, a military historian, wrote in 1999 that "America must be able to fight Iraq and North Korea, and *also* be able to fight genocide in the Balkans and elsewhere without compromising its ability to fight two major regional conflicts. *And it must be able to contemplate war with China or Russia some considerable (but not infinite) time from now* [author's emphasis]."[22]

They believe violence magically solves all disputes, even the Israeli-Palestinian morass. In a bizarre interview immediately after 9/11, Donald Kagan, the Yale classicist and right-wing ideologue who was the father of Robert and Fred, called, along with his son Fred, for the deployment of U.S. troops in Gaza so we could "take the war to these people." They have long demanded the stationing of NATO troops in Ukraine, with Robert Kagan saying that "we need to not worry that the problem is our encirclement rather than Russian ambitions." His wife, Victoria Nuland, was outed in a leaked phone conversation in 2014 with the U.S. ambassador to Ukraine, Geoffrey Pyatt, disparaging the EU and plotting to remove the lawfully elected President Viktor Yanukovych, who was close to Russia, and install compliant Ukrainian politicians in power, most of whom did eventually take power. They lobbied for U.S. troops to be sent to Syria to assist "moderate" rebels seeking to over-throw Bashar al-Assad. Instead, the intervention spawned the Caliphate. The U.S. ended up bombing the very forces they had armed, becoming Assad's de facto air force.

The Russian invasion of Ukraine, like the attacks of 9/11, is a self-fulfilling prophecy. Putin, like everyone else they target, only understands force. We can, they assure us, militarily bend Russia to our will.

"It is true that acting firmly in 2008 or 2014 would have meant risking conflict," Robert Kagan wrote in *Foreign Affairs* of Ukraine, lamenting our refusal to militarily confront Russia earlier. "But Washington is risking conflict now; Russia's ambitions have created an inherently dangerous situation. It is better for the United States to risk confrontation with belligerent powers when they are in the early stages of ambition and expansion, not after they have already consolidated substantial gains. Russia may possess a fearful nuclear arsenal, but the risk of Moscow using it is not higher now than it would have been in 2008 or 2014, if the West had intervened then. And it has always been extraordinarily small: Putin was never going to obtain his objectives by destroying himself and his country, along with much of the rest of the world."[23]

In short, don't worry about going to war with Russia, Putin won't use the bomb.

I do not know if these people are stupid or cynical or both. They are lavishly funded by the war industry. They are never dropped from the networks for their repeated idiocy. They rotate in and out of power, parked in places like the Council on Foreign Relations or the Brookings Institution, before being called back into government. They are as welcome in the Obama or Biden White House as the Bush White House. The Cold

War, for them, never ended. The world remains binary, us and them, good and evil. They are never held accountable. When one military intervention goes up in flames, they are ready to promote the next. These Dr. Strangeloves, if we don't stop them, will terminate life as we know it on the planet.

V.

The Act of Killing

I have spent time with mass killers, warlords, and death squad leaders. Some are psychopaths who relish acts of sadism, torture, and murder. But others, maybe most, see killing as a job, a profession, good for their careers and status. They enjoy playing God. They revel in the hypermasculine world of force where looting, theft, and rape are perks. They proudly refine the techniques of murder to snuff out one life after another, largely numb to the terror and cruelty they inflict. And when they are not killing, they can sometimes be disarmingly charming and gracious. Some are decent fathers and sentimental with their wives and mistresses. Some dote on their pets.

It is not the demonized, easily digestible caricature of a mass murderer that most disturbs me. It is the human being.

Joshua Oppenheimer's documentary *The Act of Killing*, which took eight years to make, explores the complex psychology of mass murderers. The film has the profundity of Gitta Sereny's book *Into That Darkness: An Examination of Conscience*, for which she carried out extensive interviews with Franz Stangl, the commandant of Treblinka, one of the Nazi extermination camps. Oppenheimer, too, presents candid confessions, interviewing some of the most ruthless murderers in Indonesia. One of these is responsible for perhaps a thousand killings, a man named Anwar Congo, who was a death squad leader in Medan, the capital of the Indonesian province North Sumatra.

The documentary also shows the killers performing reenactments of murders.

Indonesia's military, with U.S. support, in 1965 launched a yearlong campaign to ostensibly exterminate communist leaders, functionaries, party members, and sympathizers in that country. By its end, the bloodbath—much of it carried out by rogue death squads and paramilitary gangs—had decimated the labor union movement along with the intellectual and artistic class, opposition parties, university student leaders, journalists, ethnic Chinese, and many who just happened to be in the wrong spot at the wrong time. By some estimates, more than a million people were slaughtered. Many of the bodies were dumped into rivers, hastily buried, or left on roadsides.

This campaign of mass murder is still mythologized in Indonesia as an epic battle against the forces of evil and barbarity, much as U.S. popular culture for many decades mythologized our genocide of Native Americans and held up our own killers, gunmen, outlaws, and murderous cavalry units of the Old West as heroes. The onetime killers in the Indonesian war against communism are cheered at rallies today for saving the country. They are interviewed on television about the "heroic" battles they fought five decades ago. The three-million-strong Pancasila Youth—Indonesia's equivalent of the Brown Shirts or the Hitler Youth—in 1965 joined in the genocidal mayhem, and now its members, like the death squad leaders, are lionized as pillars of the nation. It is as if the Nazis had won World War II. It is as if Stangl, instead of dying in the Düsseldorf remand prison as a convicted war criminal, came to be a venerated elder statesman, as has Henry Kissinger.

There is a scene in the Oppenheimer film where Congo— who parades across the screen like a prima donna, his outsize vanity and love of fine clothing on display—is interviewed on *Special Dialogue*, a program of a state-owned television station with national coverage.

"We had to kill them," Congo, wearing a black cowboy hat adorned with a gold sheriff's star, tells the female host.

"And was your method of killing inspired by gangster films?" she asks.

"Sometimes!" Congo says. "It's like. . . "

"Amazing!" she says. "He was inspired by films!"

The audience, mostly made up of members of the Pancasila Youth in their distinctive orange and black shirts, applauds. At the start of the show, Ibrahim Sinik, a leader of the paramilitary group, lauded the Pancasila Youth as having been "at the core of the extermination."

"Each genre had its own method," Congo says. "Like in Mafia movies, they strangle the guy in the car, and dump the body. So, we did that too."

"Which means Anwar and his friends developed a new, more efficient system for exterminating communists," the woman says enthusiastically, "a system more humane, less sadistic, and without excessive force."

"Young people must remember their history," Ali Usman, a Pancasila Youth leader, interjects. "The future musn't forget the past! What's more, God must be against communists."

"Yes," the talk show host says. "God hates communists!"

There is more applause.

Oppenheimer, in the film's strangest but most psychologically astute device, persuades the killers to reenact some of the mass murders they carried out. They don costumes—they fancy themselves to be the stars of their own life movies—and what comes out in the costumed scenes of mock torture and killing is the vast disconnect between the image they have of themselves, much of it inspired by Hollywood gangster films, and the tawdry, savage, and appalling crimes they committed. These scenes include one of the old killers named Herman Koto—Koto and the other murderers refer approvingly to themselves as gangsters—done up to look like the drag queen Divine. And in these moments Oppenheimer captures the playfulness, the black humor and the comradeship that create bonds among killers. The killers stage a scene at the end of the film in which actors playing their murdered victims hang a medal around the neck of Congo—who is dressed in a long, black robe and standing in front of a waterfall—and thank him for saving the country and "killing me and sending me to heaven." This bizarre fantasy's background music, specified by Congo, is the theme from the movie *Born Free*. These same human bonds, along with the same schizophrenic self-delusion, can be glimpsed in photographs of off-duty Nazi soldiers in the book *Nein, Onkel: Snapshots from Another Front 1938–1945,* or in the photographs of off-duty SS camp guards at Auschwitz. One of the pictures in the Auschwitz album shows the SS leadership, including the commandant of Auschwitz, Rudolf Hoess, and Dr. Josef Mengele, who carried out sadistic medical experiments on children, in a raucous "sing-along" on a wooden bridge with an accordion player at Solahütte, an SS resort about twenty miles south of Auschwitz on the Sola River. Mothers and children not far away were being gassed to death, some of the one million people murdered at Auschwitz. And it is this disquieting moral fragmentation, this ability to commit mass murder and yet to see oneself as a normal, caring human being, that Oppenheimer astutely captures. The bifurcation between work and life—a bifurcation that many in the U.S. military, today's fossil fuel or health insurance industry, or Wall Street firms such as Goldman Sachs also must make—allows human beings who exploit, destroy, and kill other human beings to blot out much of their daily existence.

"I killed every Chinese I saw," Congo remembers as he tours the Chinese area of Medan in a car. "I stabbed them all! I don't remember how many, but it was dozens of Chinese. If I met them, I stabbed them. All the way to Asia Street, where I met my girlfriend's dad. Remember, I had two motives: crush the Chinese and crush my girlfriend's father, so I stabbed him, too! Because he was Chinese too! He fell into a ditch. I hit him with a brick. He sank."

"Killing is the worst crime you can do," says one of Congo's former associates. "So, the key is to find a way not to feel guilty. It's all about finding the right excuse. For example, if I'm asked to kill somebody, if the compensation is right, then of course I'll do it, and from one perspective it's not wrong. That's the perspective we must make ourselves believe. After all, morality is relative."

Congo patiently explains to Oppenheimer his technique of garroting his victims with a piece of wood, a pole, and wire, a technique he adopted to avoid the mess of excessive bleeding.

"There's probably many ghosts here, because many people were killed here," he tells Oppenheimer as they stand on a rooftop at one of his former murder spots. "They died unnatural deaths—unnatural deaths. They arrived here perfectly healthy. When they got here, they were beaten up. . . "

Congo crouches and puts his hands over his white, curly hair to imitate the last moments of his victims.

"And died," he goes on. "Dragged around. Dumped. In the early days we beat them to death. But when we did that blood spurted everywhere. It smelled awful. To avoid having blood everywhere, I used this system."

He holds a piece of wood, about two feet long, and a long wire.

"Can I demonstrate it?" he asks.

He secures the wire by wrapping one of its ends around a mounted pole. A friend, whose hands are behind his back, sits on the floor near the pole. Congo loops the wire around his friend's throat. Standing several feet away, Congo pulls lightly on the wood, attached to the other end of the wire, to show how the victim was killed.

"I've tried to forget all this by listening to good music," Congo says when he finishes his demonstration. "Dancing. I can be happy. A little alcohol. A little marijuana. A little—what do you call it?—ecstasy. Once I'd get drunk, I'd 'fly' and feel happy. Cha cha."

He begins to dance on the rooftop in his white pants and white shoes.

"He's a happy man," his friend says.

"We shoved wood in their anus until they died," Adi Zulkadry, a death squad leader, says later in the film as he is shown shopping in a mall in the capital Jakarta with his wife and daughter. "We crushed their necks with wood. We hung them. We strangled them with wire. We cut off their heads. We ran them over with cars. We were allowed to do it. And the proof is, we murdered people and were never punished. The people we killed, there's nothing to be done about it. They have to accept it. Maybe I'm just trying to make myself feel better, but it works. I've never felt guilty, never been depressed, never had nightmares."

In one scene a film crew member, his raw emotion broken by nervous laughter, says his family was on the receiving end of the terror.

"If you want a true story, I have one," the crew member volunteers.

"Tell us," Congo responds, "because everything in this film should be true."

"Well, there was a grocery store owner," the man begins hesitantly. "He was the only Chinese person in the region. To be honest, he was my stepfather. But even though he was my stepfather, I lived with him since I was a baby. At three a.m., someone knocked on our door. They called my dad. Mom said, 'It's dangerous! Don't go out.' But he went out. We heard him shout, 'Help!' And then, silence. They took him away. We couldn't sleep until morning."

"How old were you?" he is asked.

"Eleven or twelve," he answers. "I remember it well. And it's impossible to forget something like this. We found his corpse under an oil drum. The drum was cut in half and the body was under it, like this," he says as he doubles over a piece of paper to illustrate. "His head and feet were covered by sacks. But one foot poked out like this." The crew member raises one foot off the ground. "So, the same morning, nobody dared help us," he says.

"We buried him like a goat next to the main road," he says with a forced smile, as if the burial story should be amusing. "Just me and my grandfather, dragging the body, digging the grave. No one helped us. I was so young. Then, all the communist families were exiled. We were dumped in a shantytown at the edge of the jungle. That's why, to be honest, I've never been to school. I had to teach myself to read and write.

"Why should I hide this from you?" he says to the former death squad leaders, who listen with wry smiles. "This way, we can know each other better. Right? I promise I'm not trying to undermine what we've done. This isn't a criticism. It's only input for the film. I promise, I'm not criticizing you."

Congo and the other killers dismiss his story as inappropriate for the film because, as Herman Koto tells the crew member, "everything's already been planned."

"We can't include every story, or the film will never end," another death squad veteran says.

"And your story is too complicated," Congo adds. "It would take days to shoot."

The killers in the film no longer wield the power that comes with indiscriminate terror, although they periodically wander through local markets to extort money from shopkeepers, a practice Oppenheimer captures on film.

When they carry out murder reenactments, however, it triggers memories of a time when they were more than petty criminals, when they had license to do anything they wanted to anyone they chose in the name of the war against communism.

"If they're pretty, I'd rape them all, especially back then when we were the law," one of the killers remembers. "Fuck 'em! Fuck the shit out of everyone I meet."

"Especially if you get one who's only fourteen years old," he adds after he and some other death squad veterans pantomime molesting a girl and holding a knife to her throat. "Delicious! I'd say, it's gonna be hell for you but heaven on earth for me."

There are moments, usually years after their crimes, when even the most savage killers have brief flashes of self-recognition, although they usually do not reflect upon or examine these revelations. They are often, however, haunted by specific moments of murder. Oppenheimer closes his film with a reenactment scene where Congo begins by placidly describing the murders he committed at that spot and ends by retching and vomiting.

"I remember I said, 'Get out of the car,'" Congo says of one killing. "He asked, 'Where are you taking me?' Soon, he refused to keep walking, so I kicked him as hard as I could in the stomach. I saw Roshiman bringing me a machete. Spontaneously, I walked over to him and cut his head off. My friends didn't want to look. They ran back to the car. And I heard this sound. His body had fallen down. And the eyes in his head were still. . . "

He trails off.

"On the way home," he finishes, "I kept wondering, why didn't I close his eyes? And that is the source of all my nightmares. I'm always gazed at by those eyes that didn't close."

VI.

The Soldier's Tale

The soldier's tale is as old as war. It is told and then forgotten. There are always young men and women ardent for glory, seduced by the power to inflict violence and naïve enough to die for the merchants of death. The soldier's tale is the same, war after war, generation after generation.

Spenser Rapone enlisted in the Army in 2010. He attended basic training at Fort Benning, Georgia. He graduated from airborne school in February 2011 and became an Army Ranger. He watched as those around him swiftly fetishized their weapons.

"The rifle is the reification of what it means to be infantrymen," he said when I reached him by phone in Watertown, New York. "You're taught that the rifle is an extension of you. It is your life. You have to carry it at all times. The rifle made us warriors dedicated to destroying the enemy in close personal combat. At first, it was almost gleeful. We were a bunch of eighteen-year-olds, nineteen-year-olds. We had this instrument of death in our hands. We had power. We could do what 99 percent of our countrymen could not. The weapon changes you. You want to prove yourself. You want to be tested in combat. You want to deliver death. It draws you in, as much as life in the Army sucks. You start executing tactical maneuvers and battle drills. You get a certain high. It's seductive. The military beats empathy out of you. It makes you callous."

He was disturbed by what was happening around him and to him.

"When you get to RASP [the Ranger Assessment and Selection Program], you're told you not only have to understand Ranger culture and history, you have to adopt what's called an airborne Ranger in the sky," he said. "They make you go online and look at Rangers who were killed in action. You have to learn about this person and print out a copy of their obituary. It's really unsettling, the whole process. This was a class leader acting on behalf of the cadre, he said something to the effect of 'I'll give you a hint, don't pick Pat Tillman.'"

Rapone began to read about Pat Tillman, the professional football player who joined the Rangers and was killed in 2004 in Afghanistan by friendly fire, a fact that senior military officials, including Gen. Stanley A. McChrystal, who at the time was the U.S. commander in Afghanistan, covered up and replaced with a fictitious Hollywood version of death in combat with the enemy. Rapone watched the 2010 documentary *The Tillman Story* and would later read the 2006 essay "After Pat's Birthday," written by Pat's brother Kevin, who was in the Rangers with Pat. Pat Tillman, who had been in contact with Noam Chomsky, had become a critic of the war. In addition to lying to the Tillman family about Pat's death, the Army did not return, and probably destroyed, Pat's papers and diary.

"Pat Tillman showed me I could resist the indoctrination," he said. "I did not have to let the military dehumanize me and turn me into something monstrous. When I learned how his death was covered up to sell the war, it was shocking. The military wasn't interested in preserving freedom or democracy. It was only interested in protecting the profits of those in power and expanding the U.S. hegemony. I was not a Hollywood freedom fighter. I was a cog in the imperialist machine. I preyed on the poorest, most exploited people on the planet."

"We were told to 'shoot, move, and communicate,'" he said of his Ranger training. "This became our entire existence. We did not need to understand why or the larger implications. These things did not concern us."

By July 2011 he was in Khost province in Afghanistan. He was nineteen years old. He was an assistant machine gunner on an eighteen-pound weapon called the Mk-48 that is mounted on a tripod and has a fire rate of 500 to 625 rounds per minute. He carried the spare barrel, along with the ammunition, which he fed into the gun. When his fellow Rangers cleared dwellings at night, he set up a blocking position. He watched as the Rangers separated terrified men, women, and children, treating them "as if they were animals." The Rangers spoke of the Afghans as subhumans, dismissing them as "Hadjis" and "ragheads."

"A lot of the guys would say, 'I want to go out every night and kill people,'" he told me. "The Rangers are about hypermasculinity, misogyny, racism, and a hatred of other cultures."

His platoon sergeant had the hammer of Thor, a popular symbol among white supremacists, tattooed on his arm. The sergeant told new Rangers that if they saw something that upset them and wanted to speak out about it, they were "in the wrong fucking place."

Rapone left the Rangers to attend West Point in 2012. Maybe, as an officer, he could make a difference, infuse some humanity into his squads of killers. But he had his doubts.

"When I started West Point in July 2012, I encountered a

lot of similar themes I noticed in the Ranger regiment," he said. "Officers and NCOs relished the idea of being able to kill people with impunity. It's Rudyard Kipling. It's the young British soldier mentality we've seen for hundreds of years. It's hypermasculine. Even female cadets have to assimilate themselves. Any display of femininity is considered weakness. This is combined with the structural racism. They still honor Robert E. Lee at West Point. There's a barracks named after him. There's a portrait of him in the library in his Confederate uniform. In the bottom right of the portrait, in the background, is a slave."

Rapone watched with growing anger as black cadets were kicked out for infractions that did not lead to the expulsion of white cadets.

He majored in history. But he read outside of the curriculum, including Howard Zinn and Stan Goff, a former Special Forces master sergeant who had been in Vietnam, Haiti, Panama, Colombia, and Somalia and who wrote *Hideous Dream: A Soldier's Memoir of the U.S. Invasion of Haiti.*

"I realized we are the muscle for those with wealth and status," Rapone said. "I also realized I was a socialist. It was jarring."

His outspokenness and criticism saw him reprimanded.

"I almost got kicked out my senior year at West Point," he said. "At that point, I was a socialist. When you study political economy, when you study critical theory, it informs your analysis and your work. It started off as an academic position. But I thought there has to be more to this. There has to be some kind of an action to back up my theories."

He was derided as the "communist cadet." He sought out those at the military academy who suffered from discrimination, including people of color, women, and Muslims. He joined the Muslim Cadet Association, although he is not Muslim.

"I wanted to help Muslim cadets find a platform," he said. "I wanted them to know they were not forgotten. At West Point, there weren't too many people who understood or appreciated Islam or how the U.S. has ripped Islamic countries to shreds."

He helped organize an effort to provide Muslims at the academy with a proper prayer space, something that led him into heated arguments with senior administrative officials.

One professor confronted him: "I've been watching you for the past three, four years—you think you can do whatever you want."

"Yes, sir," Rapone answered, a response that resulted in his being written up for speaking back to an officer.

The professor examined his social media accounts and found Rapone was posting articles from socialist publications and criticizing U.S. policy on Syrian refugees. The teacher sent a file on Rapone to the Criminal Investigations Division and G2, or military intelligence. Rapone was interrogated by senior officers. He was issued a "punishment tour" lasting one hundred hours. He was forced to walk back and forth in the central square at West Point in his full dress uniform each week until the required hours were fulfilled.

"It looked like something out of a Monty Python sketch," he said.

He was stripped of his privileges for sixty days. His spring break was canceled. He spent spring break doing landscaping and other menial tasks to "pay off" his punishment debt. He was required to train cadets who had not passed a required event.

"At West Point, they'll maintain that hazing doesn't exist," he said, "at least the kind that was around in the fifties or sixties. But it's still hazing. You're considered a plebe when you first get to West Point. You take out upperclassmen's trash every night. You're not allowed to talk when you're outside as a plebe. You have to keep your hands balled up and walk in position of attention. If you're caught talking to a classmate, you'll get in trouble. The worst part is that those who move on from their plebe year enforce the same dehumanizing behavior, which they despised, on the new plebes."

He had experienced hazing in the Rangers, too. New Rangers were forced to fight each other and do numerous push-ups or were hog-tied and had their stomachs smacked repeatedly.

"The hazing weeds out people who won't embrace it," he said. "To resist total assimilation, a lot of people create an ironic detachment. But this ironic detachment is really another form of assimilation. It runs pretty deep. There was a guy in a leadership position who tried to kill himself when I was over-seas. There were cadets who committed suicide when I was at West Point and others who tried to commit suicide. I spent eight years in the Army. Suicide was a very tangible reality. A lot of suicides were the result of the combination of hazing and military culture, which in a sense is a form of hazing. Your drill instructor can't beat the shit out of you the way he used to, but the military still has methods to torture you emotionally."

When he graduated from West Point he was sent back to Fort Benning, where he had been a recruit six years earlier.

"Every other Friday a basic training class graduates," he said. "I would see these buzz-cut teenage boys, who had barely progressed out of puberty, being sent into the meat grinder. It was unsettling. I was being trained to lead these guys, to tell them the mission we were doing was just and right. I could not in good conscience do that. I searched for an opening. I looked for ways to leave or speak out. When the whole national anthem thing was starting up with Colin Kaepernick, putting his skin in the game, risking himself to fight against systemic racism, I thought I could at least do my part."

He posted a picture of himself in uniform with the hashtag #VeteransForKaepernick.

"Everything snowballed from there," he said. "Colin Kaepernick, for me, was linked to Pat Tillman. He too was willing to risk himself and his status to speak truth to power."

His public support of Kaepernick—along with his social media posts of photos of himself at his 2016 graduation at West Point wearing a Che Guevara T-shirt under his uniform and holding up his fist as he showed the words "Communism will win" on the inside of his cap—led to an investigation. He was given an "other than honorable" discharge for "conduct unbecoming an officer."

"The United States is almost religious about its patriotism," he said. "Military personnel are seen as infallible. You have someone like [former secretary of defense] James Mattis, who is a bona fide war criminal. He dropped bombs on a wedding ceremony in Iraq. He's responsible for overseeing many different massacres in Iraq. Or [former general and former national security adviser] H. R. McMaster. These people can't do any wrong because they've served. This reverence for the military is priming the population to accept military rule and a form of fascism or proto-fascism. That's why I felt even more compelled to get out.

"The public doesn't understand how regressive and toxic military culture is," Rapone went on. "The military's inherent function is the abuse and degradation of other people. It is designed to be a vehicle of destruction. It's fundamental to the system. Without that, it would collapse. You can't convert the military into a humanitarian force even when you use the military in humanitarian ways, such as in New Orleans during Hurricane Katrina. The military trains soldiers to see other human beings, particularly brown and black human beings, as an imminent threat.

"Of course, the military prides itself on being apolitical, which is oxymoronic. The military is the political muscle of the state. There are few things more dangerous than a soldier who thinks he or she doesn't have a political function.

"I want to implore other soldiers and military personnel, there's more to being a soldier than knowing how to fire a weapon," Rapone said. "You can take a lot of what you've learned into society and actually help. At West Point, they say they teach you to be a leader of character. They talk to you about moral fortitude. But what do we see in the military? I was blindly following orders. I was inflicting violence on the poorest people on earth. How is there any morality in that?"

Nationalists do not venerate veterans. They venerate veterans who read from the approved patriotic script. *America is the greatest and most powerful country on earth. Those we fight are depraved barbarians. Our enemies deserve death. God is on our side. Victory is assured. Our soldiers and Marines are heroes.* Deviate from this cant, no matter how many military tours you may have served, and you become despicable. The vaunted patriotism of the right wing is about self-worship. It is a raw lust for violence. It is blind subservience to the state. And it works to censor the reality of war.

When Rory Fanning, a burly veteran who served in the 2nd Army Ranger Battalion and was deployed in Afghanistan in 2002 and 2004, appeared at a Donald Trump rally during the presidential campaign in Chicago, he was wearing the top half of his combat fatigues. As he moved through the crowd, dozens of Trump supporters shouted greetings such as "Welcome home, brother" and "Thank you for your service." Then came the protest that shut down the rally. Fanning, one of the demonstrators, pulled out a flag that read, "Vets Against Racism, War and Empire."

"Immediately someone threw a drink on me," he told me. "I got hit from behind in the head three or four times. It was quite the switch, quite the pivot on me. Questioning the narrative, questioning Donald Trump's narrative, and I was suddenly out of their good graces.

"A lot of soldiers who've come back from war see themselves as anything but a hero," Fanning said. "To throw that term around loosely is dangerous. It's a way to manipulate soldiers. It buys their silence.

"Soldiers are not encouraged to talk about the realities of war when they come back," he said. "They're labeled a hero or warrior. That's a major problem. It leads to further seclusion, isolation with soldiers. We talk about the suicide rates amongst veterans—twenty-two a day. It's because we're not allowed to talk about what we saw overseas, how unjust it was, how we feel like bullies. How many innocent people have been killed since 9/11? Throwing out words like 'heroes' does a disservice to the experience of veterans and all the innocent people that have been killed since then."

War, up close, is depraved and cruel.

"What I didn't know as I entered [Afghanistan] with the 2nd Army Ranger Battalion was that the Taliban had essentially surrendered after the initial assault by the Air Force and the Special Forces," Fanning said of his first tour, which started in late 2001. "Our job was essentially to draw the Taliban back into the fight. Surrender wasn't good enough for politicians after 9/11. We wanted blood. We wanted a head count. It really didn't matter who it was. So, we'd walk up to people, people who had been occupied, involved in civil war before that, with tons of money at our disposal. We'd said, 'Hey, we will give you this amount of money if you point out a member of the Taliban.' An Afghan would say, 'Sure, absolutely. There's a member right there.' So, we go next door. We'd land in their neighbor's front yard, put a bag over every military-age person's head, whether they were a member of the Taliban or not, give the person who identified that person money. Then that person would also get that neighbor's property. In a country with as much desperation and poverty as Afghanistan you'd do anything to put money or food on your family's table. Essentially that's what we were doing. But we were also bringing people who had absolutely no stake in the fight into the war. We were creating enemies.

"I signed up after 9/11 to prevent another 9/11 from happening," he went on. "But soon after arriving in Afghanistan I realized I was only creating the conditions for more terrorist attacks. It was a hard pill to swallow. We were essentially bullies."

The disproportionate use of force on the part of the American occupation forces not only left huge numbers of civilians dead but served as a potent recruiting weapon for insurgents.

"We'd have a rocket land in our camp," said Fanning, the author of *Worth Fighting For: An Army Ranger's Journey Out of the Military and Across America*. "We wouldn't necessarily know where it came from. It came from that general direction over there. We'd call in a five-hundred-pound bomb. It would land on a village."

The terror visited on Afghans was soon replicated by the terror visited on Iraqis.

Michael Hanes was in the Marine Corps from 1994 to 2004. He was in Iraq in 2003 in the most senior recon platoon—the Marine Corps equivalent of the Navy SEALs—the 1st Force Reconnaissance Company, 1st Marine Division. He was in numerous raids.

"I was in the Iraq invasion," Hanes said. "We pushed up into Baghdad and things [became] very real for me when we began to kick in doors, place charges in doors, and rush into these homes and terrorize these people.

"Probably about 50 percent or more of the intel that we got was just dead wrong," he went on. "Busting in these doors, you come into a family's house and there's elderly women, young little girls, three, four years old, just screaming, and horrified, just terrified to where they literally soil themselves. They pee their pants. You're taking Grandma and throwing her up against the wall and interrogating her. That hits you right here. It hits you really hard. I began to ask myself, what the hell am I doing? If you happen to be a young man [in a raided home], in your early twenties or anywhere in that range where you can carry a weapon, then by mere association of being a young male, a possible insurgent, [Fedayeen Saddam] loyalist, whatever the case may be, you were taken out of the home to be interrogated. Who knows what happened to them? . . . I know [Marines] were there all night interrogating them. Who knows if they even made it back to their family?

"With the drone attacks you have a range, an outside range, where so many civilians are being killed," Hanes said. "It's a terrorist-producing factory. If you lose your child, if you lose your mother, any of your family members to this . . . we have to think about that. Put yourself in that position. If I lost my child, I would be desperate. What would you do? It's easy to understand why someone would strap a bomb to themselves and blow themselves up."

The physical brutality and violence were accompanied by the overt racism.

"We didn't refer to the people in Afghanistan as Afghans, they're Hadji," Fanning said. "This is a term of respect for someone who's gone to make the trip to Mecca, but we'd use it in a derogatory term.

"The terms 'sand nigger,' 'Hadji,' 'barbarian,' 'terrorist,' all of these things were thrown around as if the people there were subhuman," Hanes added.

The lies of the state and the wider society became painfully apparent.

A soldier or Marine who rises inside the system to denounce the hypermasculinity that glorifies violence and war, who exposes the false morality of the military, who refuses to kill in the service of imperial power, unmasks the military for what it is. And he or she, as Chelsea Manning learned, swiftly pays a very, very heavy price.

Spc. Robert Weilbacher, as a new Army combat medic stationed in South Korea, listened to stories told by combat veterans, many suffering from trauma and depression, about the routine and indiscriminate slaughter of civilians in Iraq and Afghanistan. He was horrified. He had believed the propaganda fed to him over the years. He considered himself a patriot. He had accepted the notion that the U.S. military was a force for good, intervening to liberate Iraqis and Afghans and fight terrorists. But after hearing the veterans' tales, his worldview crumbled. He began to ask questions he had not asked before. He began to think. And thinking within any military establishment is an act of subversion. He soon decided he did not want to be part of an organization that routinely snuffed out the lives of unarmed people, including children. He applied in February 2014 for a classification known as Conscientious Objector (1-0).

He instantly became a pariah within his unit. No one wanted to associate with him. He was taunted as a "traitor," "coward," "faggot," and "hippie." He was assigned to the most demeaning jobs on the base. The military bureaucracy began making him jump through hoops that he was still trying to negotiate two years later.

"I feel as if my own government is torturing me," he said when I reached him by phone in his barracks at Fort Campbell, Kentucky.

Weilbacher, twenty seven, grew up in poverty, raised by a single mother, in the inner city of Columbus, Ohio. As a student at Ohio State University, where he was a political science and English major, he started two organizations to help feed the homeless. He was an idealist. He wanted to serve humanity. And, in the warped culture in which he lived—American culture—the best way to do that was to join the military, which was organized, he thought, around "noble ideals."

"The public perception, including at Ohio State, which has a big ROTC program, is that soldiers are heroic," he said. "They're serving their country. They're in the best army in the world. I didn't question this. I watched the commercials with the climactic background music for the Marine Corps: 'the few, the proud, the Marines.' The Marines have the biggest masculine factor. I thought, I have the credentials to be a Marine officer.

"Every message given to me by popular culture was that violence was a means of conflict resolution. This was especially true in the inner city where I grew up and where there is a lack of education. Video games, such as *Call of Duty,* normalize violence. You don't realize the impact it has. Your conscience is subverted. In *Call of Duty* you get rewarded for killing— you rank up in the system. The message is, if you like *Call of Duty*, you'll like the military. And, of course, the military also incentivizes killing. If you do well at marksmanship you get rewarded with three-day passes. You only think about the points you can get from becoming an expert marksman. You don't think about the act of taking a human life. Every aspect of popular culture incentivizes violence, from television shows to movies like *American Sniper.* Killing is presented as noble. Those who kill are supposed to be heroes. And this prepares us for the military."

When he graduated from college, he signed up for Marine Officer Candidates School and was sent to Quantico, Virginia, for boot camp.

"When we marched in formation, we shouted out cadences," he said. "Most of the cadences were about killing. We shouted, 'Kill! Kill! Kill!' We shouted, 'What makes the green grass grow? Blood! Blood! Blood!' We shouted, 'AT&T. Reach out and touch someone.' The intent of OCS [Officer Candidates School] was to normalize violence, to condition us. It was very effective. Again, I didn't think about what I was doing. All I was thinking about was being a Marine Corps officer."

But four weeks into his training, in early 2012, he was injured and had to drop out. He was devastated. He did not want to begin the whole application process again with the Marines, and he enlisted in the Army in April 2013. He went to Fort Sill, Oklahoma, for basic training. He was then trained as a medic at Fort Sam Houston, Texas. He enrolled in airborne school at

Fort Benning, Georgia, and during the second week of training was injured during a practice for landing falls.

In December 2013, he was deployed to Camp Hovey in South Korea, ten miles from the border with North Korea. He was attached as a medic to the 4-7 Cavalry. He began to hear disturbing stories about the wars in the Middle East, whole families being blown up or gunned down by U.S. troops in the streets of Iraq and Afghanistan. He lived among soldiers who were suffering from post-traumatic stress disorder. Many were drinking heavily. He listened to them talk about being prescribed antidepressants by Army doctors and then being redeployed to Iraq and Afghanistan. He may have been a medic, but he was required to carry a weapon and to use it in combat. He knew that for him, to do so would be impossible. "I joined the military because I wanted to help people, to fight for the greater good," he said. "And then I learned about innocent people being routinely blown up in war. I started researching the statistics on collateral damage in Iraq and Afghanistan.

"A medic in the Army weaponizes soldiers so they can go back out and kill," he said. "When we are trained as medics, we are told that our task is to preserve fighting strength. Being a medic in the Army is not about helping the people who need it most. Treatment is first directed towards casualties that have the best chance to survive. Army medics exist to perpetuate warfare."

He started reading the Iraq Body Count website. He devoured the writings and statements of Martin Luther King Jr., Mahatma Gandhi, Noam Chomsky, Howard Zinn, Rev. John Dear, Muhammad Ali, and the Dalai Lama. He could no longer watch violent movies or play violent video games.

"I began to read about the war in Vietnam and World War II," he said. "I read about Nagasaki, Hiroshima, Agent Orange, radiation and how it's still affecting people today, how people are still dying or being born with congenital defects. I found Noam Chomsky and Howard Zinn. I had never heard of them. I guess there was a good reason I had never heard of them. I read *A People's History of the United States* by Zinn. I read *Understanding Power* by Chomsky. A lot of my influences, even though I am an atheist, came from religious figures like Gandhi, Father John Dear, and King. I read *Pilgrimage to Nonviolence*. I know why they do not tell us the truth about war. We have a volunteer army. If people knew the truth, it would decrease the numbers who want to join. I had been betrayed." Then, in early February 2014, he went online to the website of the Center on Conscience & War, led by Maria Santelli and Bill Galvin. Soon he contacted the two activists and told them he was a conscientious objector.

Everything about the military culture, from its celebration of violence and hypermasculinity to its cult of blind obedience, began to disturb him. He was disgusted by the military's exploitation of Filipina women who worked in the numerous bars and clubs near the base where he was stationed in South Korea.

"Filipina women were brought over to sing in the bars," he said. "They were great singers. They worked in bars where Korean women had been comfort women during the Japanese colonization. The bar owners took the passports of the Filipina women. . . . Soldiers bought drinks and sexual services from these exploited women. I had a big issue with that. It demonstrated a lack of values."

When he was off base, he would meditate in Buddhist temples. That helped, he said, to keep him sane.

Although Army regulations required that his application be sent to the Department of the Army Conscientious Objector Review Board (DACORB) within ninety days, it took more than two hundred days for the document to arrive there. On December 16, 2014, he was granted status as a conscientious objector and an honorable discharge. But the deputy assistant secretary of the Army for review boards, Francine Blackmon, unilaterally overrode the DACORB determination and denied his application, even though Army Regulation AR 600-43, Par. 2–8 states that a review board decision is final. In a final bid to achieve conscientious objector status, he turned to the American Civil Liberties Union.

"I have obeyed the rules during the whole process," he said. "But in the military, there is a double standard. If I do not obey the regulations, I get court-martialed. If they do not obey the regulations nothing happens. It is I who suffers. If I lose this last bid, I cannot reapply."

—·—

I spent an afternoon at the University of Massachusetts Boston with three U.S. combat veterans—two from the war in Iraq, one from the war in Vietnam—along with a Somali who grew up amid the vicious fighting in Mogadishu. All were poets or novelists.

Joshua Morgan Folmar, twenty nine, a bearded Marine Corps veteran from Alabama who participated in two hundred combat patrols in Iraq, sat next to me. He handed me his poem "Contemplating the Cotard Delusion on the Downeaster to Boston."

It begins:

Maybe I'm a walking corpse, or maybe I'm in a coma in
Germany, or Walter Reed, sucking MREs
through plastic tubes, while a few children in Haditha pick up
*   bone*
shards from the explosion and trade them like card games for
*   chocolate.*

My head droops against the window: face reflecting broken
limbs and stagnant water, blurring against the train's scratched
*   safety*
glass. And somewhere out there is my last combat patrol. And
*   somewhere out*
there, my dead friends are waiting.

Brian Turner, forty seven, who was a sergeant and infantry team leader in the 3rd Stryker Brigade in Iraq in 2003 and 2004, wrote poems in a small notebook he carried while he was there. They were published in a collection called *Here, Bullet*. One lament, called "Ashbah" (a transliteration of the Arabic word for "ghosts"), reads:

The ghosts of American soldiers
Wander the streets of Balad by night,
Unsure of their way home, exhausted,
The desert wind blowing trash
Down the narrow alleys as a voice
Sounds from the minaret, a soulful call
Reminding them how alone they are,
how lost. And the Iraqi dead,
they watch in silence from rooftops
as date palms line the shore in silhouette,
leaning toward Mecca when the dawn wind blows.[24]

None of these veterans are at ease in America.

"I live in a country that is so wealthy we can wage wars and not have to think about them," Turner said. "It is a pathology handed down from generation to generation. We talk about our military. We use words like 'heroism.' But when will we start to care about people whose names are difficult to pronounce? The list of people lost is so vast. How do I write about this and share it in a country that does not want to hear it? We want narratives that are easy and complete, ones we can process. We want wars to be recorded the way historians or people who make tombstones in cemeteries do. They give us the start, the duration, and end of the war. But for those of us who were in war it does not end. If you talk to my grandfather in Fresno, California, at some point during the day, you will be in the presence of World War II."

The worst trauma is often caused not by what combat veterans witnessed but by what they did. The moral injury. The most disturbing memories usually involve children. War creates bands of ragged, poor, dirty street urchins. The bands wander about the edges of a conflict looking for something to eat. They pick through the garbage dumps. They line the sides of roads begging convoys for food or chocolate. They attempt to sell a few pathetic items to make money. In Iraq they offered American troops "freaky"—the slang for European porn videos—whiskey or heroin (Turner said he doubted there was heroin in the packets). The children lived in fear. They saw their parents, brothers, sisters, and grandparents publicly humiliated by occupation troops. They cowered in terror during night raids as troops kicked down the doors of their houses and herded them and their families into rooms where they were made to sit, sometimes for hours, with their arms bound behind their backs with plastic ties. They warily eyed the drones circling overhead day and night, never sure when death would rain down from the sky. They saw brothers and fathers killed. They dreamed of growing up to avenge their deaths.

Children threw rocks at convoys or patrols. They worked as spotters for insurgents and at times they carried automatic weapons. And in the nightmare of a war of occupation, where every Afghan or Iraqi outside the perimeter of a base was viewed as the enemy, it was not long until children were targets. Soldiers and Marines often threw the bottles they used for urination inside their vehicles at children begging for water along the road. Children also aimed rocks at the windshields of passing trucks.

"Kids would run out and throw rocks at us," Turner said. "We were going thirty-five or forty miles an hour. A rock hits you like that, and you can be damaged for life. One of those kids smashed the windshield of one of the freight trucks. It jack-knifed, flipped, and the driver died in about ninety seconds. I remember hearing over the radio some higher-up saying, 'You are authorized to shoot children.'"

Folmar said that on occasion children fired air guns at his patrols. The Americans were unable to tell if these were toy guns or real guns and carried out confiscations to avoid killings.

"We would go to shop owners to say, 'Please don't sell these,'" he said. "One day this kid comes out and shoots at us. We yell, 'Hey!' This scares him. We take the gun out of his hand. The father comes up. He is trying to figure out what is going on. We don't have an interpreter. I was a radio operator and was usually next to my squad leader, so I was to be the Arabic translator, which is hilarious because I only had two or three weeks of training. Through hand gestures and a little Arabic, I tried to explain to the father why we had to take this gun away. We did not want his kid to die. If it were dark, we would not know if that was [an air] gun or not. The father did not understand. I don't blame him. I had crappy Arabic. My squad leader was exhausted and pissed. He pulled out his M9 service pistol and put it in the father's face. He said, 'Do you understand this?'"

On some days children were to be courted, on other days threatened. The children could never tell how troops would respond.

"The rules of engagement constantly changed," Folmar said. On some days it was shoot anything in sight. Then it would be about hearts and minds. Giving out chocolate. Giving stuff to schools that were blown to bits. We would carry candy. Then the next week the kids would scream 'Chocolate! Chocolate!' and we would have been told to keep the kids away.

"We were on patrol, and I was pegged by a rock on the head," Folmar said. "The father comes out of nowhere and starts whacking the shit out of this kid. We were all laughing. But later on, I thought what kind of world must you live in where the father is beating the crap out of his son? It was partly out of respect. But it was also about recognizing that your kid can be killed for throwing a rock.

"There was this point where we really started, I don't want to say hating the children, but we were exasperated. We became cynical. There became a moment where we realized we were stuck in it. That what we were doing was just creating a new generation that would hate each other. It never got to the point where anyone in my unit said, 'Let's just kill them,' but there became a moment when we all felt 'What is the point?' We were making them mad. They are going to hate us. It's just going to continue."

Folmar said that when U.S. troops inspected trucks at checkpoints, many of the vehicles were carrying corpses to be buried, and it was not uncommon to see corpses of children. "It was a regular thing," he said.

The war in Vietnam had many of the same dynamics, with the added abuse of thousands of girls who populated brothels outside the vast military bases and in cities like Saigon.

George Kovach, sixty six, the third combat veteran in the group, was wounded in Vietnam with a friend from his unit. When they were being evacuated by helicopter, his friend died next to him. He still fights off depression and thoughts of suicide.

"I remember soldiers chucking C-ration cans at the heads of children—I know I did, and sometimes it was worse," he said. "There were lots of kids that were camp followers. In Vietnam these kids would point you out [to the Viet Cong]. When we left on patrol, we were always worried the kids would report our movements."

Boyah J. Farah, thirty six, endured the war in Somalia as a teenager with his mother. He was the oldest of five siblings. During our Boston meeting he listened in silence to the stories of the military veterans, remembering, he said, what it was like to be on the other side of the divide. He quoted an African proverb: "When the elephants fight, it is the grass that suffers."

"Militia would come into the city and take everything," Farah said. "Then that militia would be defeated. A new militia would come in. Each militia that came in was hungry, hungry to steal, hungry to rape. They would take everything, including our small amount of rice. If there were food on the stove, they would take it. As soon as you thought you had adapted, new militias appeared."

Turner turned to Farah. "I used to kick in people's doors,"

he said to him. "My job was to do raids night after night after night. I wonder about this now. And this is difficult for me to write about. I can write about what it is like to kick in a door. But . . . I wonder about the kids that were in some of those houses. When the war is over, do you feel comfortable in your own house? Do you feel safe?"

Farah shook his head. "Once you go through that experience it never goes away," he answered. "It is like the experience you had [in combat]. I came here [to the United States] in 1993. I never feel completely safe. I never get used to the Fourth of July. As soon as I hear the boom sound [of the fireworks], the war comes. Even the bang of a door brings it back.

"I escaped," Farah said. "I got educated. I came to a country at peace. But most of my friends did not make it to a peaceful country. They remained behind. And those left behind lived only for revenge. When I was in the refugee camp in Kenya, I heard my friend, whose father was killed, pray out loud and say: 'God, I don't know what you have planned for me. But I am going back to kill a hundred men.' He was sixteen or seventeen. I am sure he went back. I am sure he killed. I doubt he is alive."

"The hardest thing to write about is love," Turner said. "It comes across as sappy. This inability to write about love is part of the pathology of war. Writing about war is easy. War is addictive. I am drawn to that sort of frenetic experience. But what I want is love. I want to write poems for my wife. But when I try, they are not good."

Folmar voiced a similar thought. "I understand violence," he said. "I can put it on a page. I can do it well. But it is the love that I can't do. How am I supposed to write about love? Especially when I have these other things to write about. My wife asked me, 'You write about all these sad things. When are you going to write about me?' I have to get the other stuff out first. I am hoping I will get it out. I am hoping it will go away."

VII.

Existential Crisis

The crisis faced by combat veterans returning from war is not simply a struggle with trauma and alienation. It is often, for those who can slice through the suffering to self-awareness, an existential crisis. War exposes the lies we tell ourselves about ourselves. It rips open the hypocrisy of our religions and secular institutions. Those who return from war have learned something which is often incomprehensible to those who have stayed home. We are not a virtuous nation. God and fate have not blessed us above others. Victory is not assured. War is neither glorious nor noble. And we carry within us the capacity for evil we ascribe to those we fight.

The words these prophets speak are painful. We, as a nation, prefer to listen to those who speak from the patriotic script. We prefer to hear ourselves exalted. If veterans speak of terrible wounds, visible and invisible, of lies told to make them kill, of evil committed in our name, we fill our ears with wax. Not *our* boys, we say, not them, bred in our homes, endowed with goodness and decency. For if it is easy for them to murder, what about us? And so, it is simpler and more comfortable not to hear. We do not listen to the cascades of angry words from their lips, wishing only that they would calm down, be reasonable, get some help, and go away. We, the deformed, brand our prophets as madmen. We cast them into the desert. This is why so many veterans are estranged and enraged. This is why so many succumb to suicide or addictions.

In his book *Out of the Night: The Spiritual Journey of Vietnam Vets*, the Rev. William P. Mahedy, who was a Catholic chaplain in Vietnam, tells of a soldier, a former altar boy, who says to him: "Hey, Chaplain . . . how come it's a sin to hop into bed with a *mama-san* but it's okay to blow away gooks out in the bush?"[25]

"Consider the question that he and I were forced to confront on that day in a jungle clearing," Mahedy wrote. "How is it that a Christian can, with a clear conscience, spend a year in a war zone killing people and yet place his soul in jeopardy by spending a few minutes with a prostitute? If the New Testament prohibitions of sexual misconduct are to be stringently interpreted, why, then, are Jesus' injunctions against violence not binding in the same way? In other words, what does the commandment 'Thou shalt not kill' really mean?"[26]

Military chaplains, a majority of whom are evangelical Christians, defend the life of the unborn, tout America as a Christian nation, support the death penalty, and eagerly bless the wars in Iraq and Afghanistan as holy crusades. The hollowness of their morality, the staggering disconnect between the values they claim to promote, is ripped open in war.

There is a difference between killing someone who is trying to kill you and taking the life of someone who does not have the power to harm you. The first is killing. The second is murder. But in any war where the enemy is elusive and rarely seen, murder occurs far more often than killing. Families are

massacred in air strikes. Children are gunned down in blis-
tering suppressing fire laid down in neighborhoods after an
improvised explosive device goes off near a convoy. Artillery
shells obliterate homes. And no one stops to look. The dead
and maimed are left behind.

The failure of nearly all our religious institutions—whose
texts are unequivocal about murder—to address the essence of
war has rendered them useless. These institutions have little or
nothing to say in wartime, because the god they worship is a
false god, one that promises victory to those who obey the law
and believe in the manifest destiny of the nation.

We all have the capacity to commit evil. It takes little to
unleash it. For those of us who have been to war, this is the
awful knowledge that is hardest to digest, the knowledge that
the line between the victims and the victimizers is razor-thin,
that human beings find a perverse delight in destruction and
death, and that few can resist the pull. At best, most of us
become silent accomplices.

Wars may have to be fought to ensure survival, but they
are always tragic. They always bring to the surface the worst
elements of any society, those who have a penchant for violence and a lust for absolute power. They turn the moral order
upside down. It was the criminal class that first organized the
defense of Sarajevo. When these goons were not manning roadblocks to hold off the besieging Bosnian Serb army, they were
looting, raping, and killing the Serb residents in the city. And
those politicians who speak of war as an instrument of power,
those who wage war but do not know its reality, those powerful statesmen—the Henry Kissingers, Robert McNamaras,
Donald Rumsfelds, the Dick Cheneys—those who treat war as
part of the great game of nations, are as amoral as the religious

stooges who assist them. And when the wars are over, what they have to say to us in their thick memoirs about war is also fatuous and empty.

"In theological terms, war is sin," wrote Mahedy. "This has nothing to do with whether a particular war is justified or whether isolated incidents in a soldier's war were right or wrong. The point is that war as a human enterprise is a matter of sin. It is a form of hatred for one's fellow human beings. It produces alienation from others and nihilism, and it ultimately represents a turning away from God."[27]

The young soldiers and Marines do not plan or organize the war. They do not seek to justify it or explain its causes. They are taught to believe. The symbols of the nation and religion are interwoven. The will of God becomes the will of the nation. This trust is forever shattered.

Society's institutions, including our religious institutions, which mold us into compliant citizens, are unmasked. This betrayal is so deep that many never find their way back to faith in the nation or in God. They nurse a self-destructive anger and resentment, understandable and justified, but also crippling. Ask a combat veteran struggling to piece his or her life together about God, and watch the raw vitriol and pain pour out. They have seen into the corrupt heart of America, into the emptiness of its most sacred institutions, into our staggering hypocrisy, and those of us who refuse to heed their words become complicit in the evil they denounce.

All troops, when they occupy and battle insurgent forces, as in Ukraine, Iraq, Afghanistan, Syria, Gaza, or Vietnam, are placed in what the psychiatrist Robert Jay Lifton calls "atrocity-producing situations." In this environment, surrounded by a hostile population, a simple act such as going to a store to buy a can of Coke means you can be killed. This constant fear and stress push troops to view everyone around them as the enemy. This hostility is compounded when the enemy is elusive, shadowy, and hard to find. The rage soldiers feel after a roadside bomb explodes, killing or maiming their comrades, or when a helicopter or troop transport plane is shot down and everyone inside is killed, is one that is easily directed over time to innocent civilians, who are fused with the insurgents. It is a short psychological leap, but a massive moral leap. It is a leap from killing to murder. Soldiers and Marines swiftly become socialized to murder.

"This unit sets up this traffic control point and this eighteen-year-old kid is on top of an armored Humvee with a .50 caliber machine gun," recalled Geoffrey Millard, who served in Tikrit with the 42nd Infantry Division. "And this car speeds at him pretty quick and he makes a split-second decision that that's a suicide bomber, and he presses the butterfly trigger and puts two hundred rounds in less than a minute into this vehicle. It killed the mother, a father, and two kids. The boy was aged four and the daughter was aged three.

"And they briefed this to the general," Millard said, "and they briefed it gruesome. I mean, they had pictures. They briefed it to him. And this colonel turns around to this full division staff and says, 'If these fucking Hadjis learned to drive, this shit wouldn't happen.'"[28]

Those who come back from war, like Millard, suffer not only delayed reactions to stress, but a crisis of faith. The God they knew, or thought they knew, failed them. The church or the synagogue or the mosque, which promised redemption by serving God and country, did not prepare them for the betrayal of this civic religion, for the capacity we all have for atrocity.

"And then, you know, my sort of sentiment of what the fuck are we doing, that I felt that way in Iraq," said Sgt. Ben Flanders, who estimated that he ran hundreds of convoys in Iraq. "It's the sort of insanity of it and the fact that it reduces it. Well, I think war does anyway, but I felt like there was this enormous reduction in my compassion for people, the only thing that wound up mattering is myself and the guys that I was with. And everybody else be damned, whether you are an Iraqi, I'm sorry, I'm sorry you live here, I'm sorry this is a terrible situation, and I'm sorry that you have to deal with all of this, you know, army vehicles running around and shooting, and these insurgents and all this stuff."[29]

"The first briefing you get when you get off the plane in Kuwait, and you get off the plane and you're holding a duffel bag in each hand," Millard remembered. "You've got your weapon slung. You've got a web sack on your back. You're dying of heat. You're tired. You're jet-lagged. Your mind is just full of goop. And then, you're scared on top of that, because, you know, you're in Kuwait, you're not in the States anymore . . . so fear sets in, too. And they sit you into this little briefing room and you get this briefing about how, you know, you can't trust any of these fucking Hadjis, because all these fucking Hadjis are going to kill you. And Hadji is always used as a term of disrespect and usually, with the 'f' word in front of it."[30]

War empowers soldiers to destroy not only things but human beings, to revoke another person's charter to live on this earth. The frenzy of this destruction—and when unit discipline breaks down, or there was no unit discipline to begin with, frenzy is the right word—sees armed bands crazed by the poisonous elixir the power to bring about the obliteration of others delivers. All things, including human beings, become objects—objects to either gratify or destroy or both.

"A lot of guys really supported that whole concept that, you know, if they don't speak English and they have darker skin, they're not as human as us, so we can do what we want," said Josh Middleton, who served in the 82nd Airborne in Iraq. "And you know, when twenty-year-old kids are yelled at back and forth at Bragg and we're picking up cigarette butts and getting yelled at every day to find a dirty weapon. But over here, it's like life and death. And forty-year-old Iraqi men look at us with fear and we can—do you know what I mean?—we have this power that you can't have. That's really liberating. Life is just knocked down to this primal level of, you know, you worry about where the next food's going to come from, the next sleep or the next patrol and to stay alive."[31]

Camilo Mejía, while on active duty, applied to become a conscientious objector. He was disgusted by the racism and contempt the soldiers and officers in his unit had for Arabs, Everything was ridiculed, "Hadji food," "Hadji homes," and "Hadji music" and "Hadji toilets," holes in the floor, which meant you would be "shitting like dogs." He took part in what he considered senseless brutality. He went on house raids where families were needlessly terrorized by soldiers bursting into their homes, stripping them naked, screaming at them in English, and forcing them to stand for hours outside in the baking heat. Soldiers stole food and valuables from the houses as families, including children, watched, huddled in fear. The behavior of the soldiers enraged Iraqis and fueled the insurgency.

"I experienced horrible confusion," Mejía remembers, "not knowing whether I was more afraid for the detainees or for what would happen to me if I did anything to help them."[32]

"After we arrested drivers," he recalled, "we would choose whichever vehicles we liked, fuel them from confiscated jerry cans, and conduct undercover presence patrols in the impounded cars.

"But to this day I cannot find a single good answer as to why I stood by idly during the abuse of those prisoners, except, of course, my own cowardice," he said.[33]

Iraqi families were routinely fired upon when they drove too close to checkpoints or did not slow their car to a crawl as they approached one of the numerous roadblocks. Mejía saw a father decapitated by a .50-caliber machine gun in front of his small son in their car, although by then, Mejía noted, "this sort of killing of civilians had long ceased to arouse much interest or even comment."[34] Soldiers for sport shot holes into cans of gasoline being sold alongside the road and then tossed incendiary grenades into the pools to set them ablaze. "It's fun to shoot shit up," a soldier said. Some opened fire on small children throwing rocks. A blast from an improvised explosive device resulted in soldiers firing wildly with heavy M-240 Bravo machine guns, AT-4 launchers, and Mark 19s, machine guns that spit out grenades, into houses alongside the road, leaving behind scores of wounded and dead, dismissed as "collateral damage."

"We would drive on the wrong side of the highway to reduce the risk of being hit by an IED," Mejía said of the deadly roadside bombs. "This forced oncoming vehicles to move to one side of the road, and considerably slowed down the flow of traffic. In order to avoid being held up in traffic jams, where someone could roll a grenade under our trucks, we would simply drive up on sidewalks, running over garbage cans and even hitting civilian vehicles to push them out of the way. Many of the soldiers would laugh and shriek at these tactics."[35]

Mejía and his squad, struggling to contain a crowd of Iraqis protesting the occupation, opened fire on an Iraqi holding a grenade. They riddled the man's body with bullets. Mejía checked his clip afterwards. He had put eleven rounds into the young man.

"The frustration that resulted from our inability to get back at those who were attacking us," Mejía wrote later, "led to tactics that seemed designed simply to punish the local population that was supporting them."[36]

Soldiers abused the corpses of Iraqis they killed. Soldiers, in one incident, laughed as an Iraqi corpse fell out of the back of a truck.

"Take a picture of me and this motherfucker," one of the soldiers who had been in Mejía's squad in third platoon said, putting his arm around the corpse.

The shroud fell away from the body, revealing a young man wearing only his pants. There was a bullet hole in his chest.

"Damn, they really fucked you up, didn't they!?" the soldier laughed.

The scene was witnessed by the dead man's brothers and cousins.[37]

Senior officers, who rarely left their fortified compounds, sent their troops on futile patrols in the quest to be awarded Combat Infantry Badges. A Combat Infantry Badge, Mejía said, "was essential to their further progress up the officer ranks." This pattern meant that "very few high-ranking officers actually got out into the action, and lower-ranking officers were afraid to contradict them when they were wrong." When the badges, bearing an emblem of a musket with the hammer dropped, resting on top of an oak wreath, arrived the senior officers immediately brought in Iraqi tailors to sew the badges on the left breast pockets of their desert combat uniforms.[38]

"This was one occasion when our leaders led from the front," Mejía noted bitterly. "They were among the first to visit the tailors to get their little patches of glory sewn next to their hearts."[39]

The violence was senseless.

"I mean, if someone has a fan, they're a white-collar family," said Phillip Chrystal, who carried out raids on Iraqi homes in Kirkuk. "So, we get started on this day, this one, in particular. And it starts with the psy ops [psychological operations] vehicles out there, you know, with the big speakers playing a message in Arabic or Farsi or Kurdish or whatever they happen to be, saying, basically, saying put your weapons, if you have them, next to the front door in your house. Please come outside, blah, blah, blah, blah. And we had Apaches flying over for security, if they're needed, and it's also a good show of force. And we were running around, and we'd done a few houses by this point, and I was with my platoon leader, my squad leader, and maybe a couple other people, but I don't really remember.

"And we were approaching this one house, and this farming area, they're, like, built up into little courtyards," he said. "So, they have like the main house, common area. They have like a kitchen and then they have like a storage-shed-type deal. And we were approaching, and they had a family dog. And it was barking ferociously because it was doing its job. And my squad leader, just out of nowhere, just shoots it. And he didn't— motherfucker—he shot it and it went in the jaw and exited out. So, I see this dog—and I'm a huge animal lover. I love animals—and this dog has like these eyes on it and he's running around spraying blood all over the place. And like, you know, the family is sitting right there with three little children and a mom, and a dad, horrified. And I'm at a loss for words. And so,

I yell at him. I'm like what the fuck are you doing. And so, the dog's yelping. It's crying out without a jaw. And I'm looking at the family, and they're just scared. And so, I told them, I was like fucking shoot it, you know. At least, kill it, because that can't be fixed. It's suffering. And I actually get tears from just saying this right now, but—and I had tears then, too—and I'm looking at the kids and they are so scared. So, I got the interpreter over with me and, you know, I get my wallet out and I gave them twenty bucks, because that's what I had. And, you know, I had him give it to them and told them that I'm so sorry that fucker did that. Which was very common.

"Was a report ever filed about it?" he asked. "Was anything ever done? Any punishment ever dished out? No, absolutely not."[40]

Klaus Theweleit, in his two volumes titled *Male Fantasies*, which draw on the bitter alienation of demobilized veterans in Germany following the end of World War I, argues that a militarized culture attacks all that is culturally defined as the feminine, including love, gentleness, compassion, and acceptance of difference. It sees any sexual ambiguity as a threat to male "hardness" and the clearly defined roles required by the militarized state. The continued support for our permanent war economy, the continued elevation of military values as the highest good, sustains the perverted ethic, rigid social roles, and emotional numbness that Theweleit explored.

Fascism, Theweleit argued, is not so much a form of government or a particular structuring of the economy or a system, but the creation of potent slogans and symbols that form a kind of psychic economy which places sexuality in the service of destruction. The "core of all fascist propaganda is a battle against everything that constitutes enjoyment and pleasure,"

Theweleit wrote.[41] And our culture, while it disdains the name of fascism, embraces its dark ethic.

New York Times columnist Thomas Friedman, interviewed in 2003 by Charlie Rose, spoke in this sexualized language of violence to justify the war in Iraq:

"What they needed to see was American boys and girls going house to house, from Basra to Baghdad, and basically saying, 'Which part of this sentence don't you understand?'" Friedman said. "'You don't think, you know, we care about our open society? You think this bubble fantasy, we're just gonna let it grow? Well, *suck on this*.' That, Charlie, was what this war was about. We could have hit Saudi Arabia, it was part of that bubble. Could have hit Pakistan. We hit Iraq because we could."[42]

The philosopher Theodor Adorno wrote that exclusive preoccupation with personal concerns and indifference to the suffering of others beyond the self-identified group made fascism and the Holocaust possible.

"The inability to identify with others was unquestionably the most important psychological condition for the fact that something like Auschwitz could have occurred in the midst of more or less civilized and innocent people," Adorno wrote. "What is called fellow traveling was primarily business interest: one pursues one's own advantage before all else, and simply not to endanger oneself, does not talk too much. That is a general law of the status quo. The silence under the terror was only its consequence. The coldness of the societal monad, the isolated competitor, was the precondition, as indifference to the fate of others, for the fact that only very few people reacted. The torturers know this, and they put it to test ever anew."[43]

VIII.

Corpses

Jessica Goodell grew up in a middle-class home near Chautauqua Lake in upstate New York. Her father was a lawyer, and her mother worked at home. But her "universe fractured" when she was sixteen and her parents divorced. She could barely continue "the motions of everyday existence." She was accepted at Ithaca College her senior year, but just before graduation a uniformed Marine came to her high school. He told her he had come to find "tough men."

"What about tough women?" she asked.

By that afternoon she was in the Marine recruiting office. She told the recruiter she wanted to be part of a tank crew but was informed that women were prohibited from operating tanks. She saw a picture of a Marine standing next to a vehicle with a huge hydraulic arm and two smaller forklift arms. She signed up to be a heavy equipment mechanic, although she knew nothing about heavy equipment.

Three years later, while stationed at the Marine Corps Air Ground Combat Center in the desert town of Twentynine Palms, California, she volunteered to serve in the Marine Corps' first official Mortuary Affairs unit, at Al Taqaddum Airbase in Iraq. Her job, for eight months, was to "process" dead Marines—collect and catalog their bodies and personal effects.

She put the remains in body bags and placed the bags in metal boxes. Before being shipped to Dover Air Force Base, the boxes were stored, often for days, in a refrigerated unit known as a "reefer." Her unit processed six suicides. The suicide notes, she told me, almost always cited hazing. Marines who were overweight or unable to do the physical training were subjected to withering verbal and physical abuse. They were called "fat nasties" and "shit bags." They were assigned to other Marines as "slaves." Many were forced to run until they vomited or to bear-crawl—walk on all fours—the length of a football field and back. This would be followed by sets of monkey fuckers—bending down, grabbing the ankles, crouching like a baseball catcher, and then standing up again—and other exercises that went on until the Marines collapsed.

Goodell's unit was sent to collect the bodies of the Marines who killed themselves.

"We went through everything," she told me. "We would get everything that the body had on it when the Marine died. Everyone had a copy of the Rules of Engagement in their left breast pocket. You found notes that people had written to each other. You found lists. Lists were common, the things they wanted to do when they got home or food they wanted to eat. The most difficult was pictures. Everyone had a picture of their wife or their kids or their family. And then you had the younger kids who might be eighteen years old and they had prom pictures or pictures next to what I imagine were their first cars. Everyone had a spoon in their flak jacket. There were pens and trash and wrappers and MRE food. All of it would get sent back [to the Marines' homes]. We all had the idea that at any point this could be us on the table. I think Marines thought that we went over there to die. And so, people wrote letters saying, 'If I die, I want you to know I love you.' 'I want my car to go to my younger brother.' Things like that. They carried those letters on their bodies. We had a Marine that we processed and going through his wallet he had a picture of a sonogram of a fetus his wife had sent him. And a lot of Marines had tattooed their vital information under an armpit. It was called a meat tag.

"Some things were not uncommon enough, like a suicide note," she continued. "We had a Marine who was in a port-a-john when he blew his face off. We had another Marine who shot himself through the neck. Often, they would do it in the corner of a bunker or an abandoned building. We had a couple that did it in port-a-johns. We had to go in and peel and pull off chunks of flesh and brain tissue that had sprayed the walls. We sent the suicide notes home with the bodies. We had the paperwork to do fingerprinting, but we started getting bodies in which there weren't any hands, or we would get bodies that were just meat. Very quickly it became irrelevant to have a fingerprinting page to fill out. By the time we would get a body it might have been a while and rigor mortis had already set in. Their hands were usually clenched as if they were still holding their rifle. We received a call one day that an IED exploded under an Army convoy that was crossing a bridge. It had literally shot a seven-ton truck over the side and down into a ravine. We had on our white plastic suits and face masks and our gloves, and I was with a Marine named Pineda. I was coming around the Humvee, and there was a spot on the ground that was a circle. I looked at it and I thought well, something must have exploded here, or near here. I looked in and saw a boot. Then I noticed the boot had a foot in it. The body of the assistant driver was trapped in the vehicle. All of his body was in the vehicle; we had to crawl in there to get it out. Pineda and I pulled the burnt upper torso from the truck. Then we removed a leg. Some of the remains had to be scooped up by putting our hands together as though we were cupping water. That was very common. A lot of the deaths were from IEDs or explosions. You might have an upper torso, but you needed to scoop the rest of the remains into a body bag. It was very common to have body bags that when you picked them up, they would sink in the middle because they were filled with flesh."

She wrote in her 2011 memoir, *Shade It Black: Death and After in Iraq*:

> Our platoon was to the Marines what the Marines are to much of America: We did things that had to be done but no one wanted to know about. The other Marines knew what we did, but they did not want to think it could happen to them. We were different from the other Marines. The smell of death permeated our clothes, hair, skin, fingers. Our cammies would be stained with blood or with brains. When you scoop up the meat it often would get on the cuffs of our shirts. You could smell it, even after you took off your gloves. We weren't washing our cammies every day. Your cuff comes to your face when you eat. We had a constant smell like rotten meat, which I guess is what it was since often the bodies had been in the sun and the heat for a long time.
>
> The sun does horrible things to dead skin. It makes the skin slide off the body; when the man is lifted, the skin detaches itself from the layer beneath and slides

around on itself. We lost two men from our original platoon who said that they couldn't, or wouldn't, do it anymore, and left. One would take a box of NyQuil tablets every day and drink as much cold medicine as he could get his hands on, but that only seemed to make matters worse. He had gone out on a particularly difficult convoy, to a tank that had been blown up, obliterated except for the tracks, leaving thousands of body parts, fingers and testicles and ears and tiny scraps of tissue to be collected. It was shortly after that when I heard that he was medevacked out.

One of our tougher days occurred after a platoon of Marines was on a security patrol. When they finished, they did a head count and realized that two Marines were missing. An investigation charted the route the platoon had followed, and we were sent out to find them. At one point, the Marines were walking along the shore of a lake. Navy divers accompanied us, and soon they found the two. By the time they were pulled from the lake, they had been submerged for quite a while. The water made the remains swell. One man was so bloated and misshapen that we had difficulty carrying him properly in the litter. His neck was as wide as his bloated head, and his stomach jutted out like a barrel. His testicles were the size of cantaloupes. His face was white and puffy and thick. Not fat, but thick. It was unreal. He looked like a movie prop, with thick, gray, waxy skin, and the thick purple lips. We couldn't stop looking at these bodies because they were so out of proportion and so disfigured and because, still, they looked like us.

One time, several Marines were killed at once. Our Marines returned to the bunker with seven or eight body bags filled with flesh. We had clean body bags set up so we could sort the flesh. Sometimes things come in with nametags. Or sometimes one is Hispanic, and you could tell who was Hispanic and who was the white guy. We tried separating flesh. It was ridiculous. We would open a body bag and there was nothing but vaporized flesh. There were not four hands or a whole leg in a bag. We tried to distribute the mush evenly throughout the bags. We had the last body bag come in. We opened it up and it was filled with the heads. I looked at four before looking away. Not only did we have to look at them, we had to pick them up and figure out who it belonged to. The eyes were looking back at us. We saw so much throughout the eight months of the program, and we managed to get used to a lot of it. But the heads worked the other way. They affected us more strongly as time passed.[44]

On another night, she and Pineda were assigned to process a body. Goodell wrote:

He was fully dressed in his cammies and his whole body was intact. His hands were lying folded across his stomach. I looked at his chest and saw that it was moving. I spun around and hid. He wasn't dead. He wasn't dead, and I didn't know what to do. The doc said, "Just wait." "Just wait? Wait for what?" I asked. "There's nothing we can do," the doc said. "Just wait." "People don't wait for this sort of thing," I protested to

Pineda. "What are we waiting for? What if this Marine was your brother, would we wait?" Pineda and I stood there for a couple of minutes that passed like hours, until the young man died. I stormed out of the bunker—I just walked out, which is something Marines cannot do. But I was so angry. And I was just a kid, who two or three years earlier had been playing the saxophone in high school band.[45]

IX

When the Bodies Come Home

Carlos Arredondo, a native Costa Rican, stands in a parking lot of a Holiday Inn in Portland, Maine, next to his green Nissan pickup truck. The truck, its tailgate folded down, carries a flag-draped coffin and is adorned with pictures of his son, Lance Cpl. Alexander S. Arredondo, twenty, a Marine killed in Iraq in 2004. The truck and a trailer he pulls with it have become a mobile shrine to his boy. He drives around the country, with the aid of donations, evoking a mixture of sympathy and hostility. There are white crosses with the names of other boys killed in the war. Combat boots are nailed to the side of the display. There is a wheelchair, covered in colored ribbons, fixed to the roof of the cab. There is Alex's military uniform and boots, poster-size pictures of the young Marine shown on the streets of Najaf, in his formal Marine portrait, and then lying, his hands folded in white gloves, in his coffin. A metal sign on the back of the truck bears a gold star and reads: USMC L/CPL ALEXANDER S. ARREDONDO.

"This is what happens every week to some family in America," says Carlos. "This is what war does. And this is the grief and pain the government does not want people to see."

Alex, from a working-class immigrant family, was lured into the military a month before September 11, 2001. The Marine recruiters made the usual appeals to patriotism, promised that he would be trained for a career, go to college, and become a man. They included a $10,000 sign-on bonus. Alex was in the Marine units that invaded Iraq. His father, chained to the news reports, listening to the radio and two televisions at the same time, was increasingly distraught. "I hear nothing about my son for days and days," he says. "It was too much, too much, too much for parents."

Alex, in August 2004, was back in Iraq for a second tour. In one of his last phone calls, Alex told him: "Dad, I call you because, to say, you know, we've been fighting for many, many days already, and I want to tell you that I love you and I don't want you to forget me." His father answered, "Of course I love you, and I don't want—I never forget you." The last message the family received was an email around that time which read: "Watch the news online. Check the news and tell everyone that I love them."

Twenty days later, on August 25, a U.S. government van pulled up in front of Carlos's home in Hollywood, Florida. It was Carlos's forty-fourth birthday He was expecting a birthday call from Alex. "I saw the van and thought maybe Alex had come home to surprise me for my birthday, or maybe they were coming to recruit my other son, Brian," he says.

Three Marine officers climbed out of the van. One asked, "Are you Carlos Arredondo?" He answered yes.

"I'm sorry, we're here to notify you about the death of Lance Cpl. Arredondo," one of the officers told him. Alex was the 968th soldier or Marine to be killed in the Iraq war.

"I tried to process this in my head," Carlos says. "I never

hear that. I remember how my body felt. I got a rush of blood to my body. I felt like it's the worst thing in my life. It is my worst fear. I could not believe what they were telling me."

Carlos turned and ran into the house to find his mother, who was in the kitchen making him a birthday cake. "I cried, 'Mama! Mama! They are telling me Alex got killed! Alex got killed! They kill Alex! They kill Alex! They kill Alex!'" His mother crumbled in grief. Carlos went to the large picture of his son in the living room and held it. Carlos asked the Marines to leave several times over the next twenty minutes, but the Marines refused, saying they had to wait for his wife. "I did this because I was in denial. I think if they leave none of this will happen." Crazed and distraught with grief, the father went into his garage and took out five gallons of gasoline and a propane torch. He walked past the three Marines in their dress blues and began to smash the windows of the government van with a hammer.

"I went into the van," he says. "I poured gasoline on the seats. I poured gasoline on the floor and in the gas tank. I was, like, looking for my son. I was screaming and yelling for him. I remember that one day he left in a van and now he's not there. I destroy everything. The pain I feel is the pain of what I learned from war. I was wearing only socks and no shoes. I was wearing shorts. The fumes were powerful, and I could not breathe no more, even though I broke the windows."

As Carlos stepped out of the van, he ignited the propane torch inside the vehicle. It started a fire that "threw me from the driver's seat backwards onto the ground." His clothes caught fire. It felt "like thousands of needles stabbing into my body." He ran across the street and fell onto the grass. His mother followed him and pulled off his shirt and socks, which were on fire, as he screamed, "Mama! Mama! My feet are burning! My feet are burning!" The Marines dragged him away and he remembers one of them saying, "The van is going to blow! The van is going to blow!" The van erupted in a fireball, and the rush of hot air, he says, swept over him. The Marines called a fire truck and an ambulance. Carlos sustained second- and third-degree burns over 26 percent of his body. As I talk to him in the Portland parking lot, he shows me the burn scars on his legs. The government chose not to prosecute him.

"I wake up in the hospital two days later and I was tied with tubes in my mouth," he says. "When they take the tubes out, I say, 'I want to be with my son. I want to be with my son.' Somebody was telling me my son had died. I get very emotional. I kept saying 'I want to be with my son' and they think I want to commit suicide."

He had no health insurance. His medical bills soon climbed to $55,000. On September 2, 2004, Carlos, transported in a stretcher, attended his son's wake at the Rodgers Funeral Home in Jamaica Plain, Massachusetts. He lifted himself, with the help of those around him, from his stretcher, and when he reached his son's open casket, he kissed his child. "I held his head and when I put my hands in the back of his head, I felt the huge hole where the sniper bullet had come out," he says. "I climbed into the casket. I lay on top of my son. I apologized to him because I did not do enough to avoid this."

Arredondo began to collect items that memorialized his son's life. He tacked them to his truck. A funeral home in Boston donated a casket to the display. He began to attend anti-war events, at times flying the American flag upside down to signal distress. He has taken his shrine to the mall in Washington, D.C., and Times Square in New York City. He has traveled throughout the country presenting to the public a visual expression of death and grief. He has placed some of his son's favorite childhood toys and belongings in the coffin, including a soccer ball, a pair of shoes, a baseball, and a Winnie the Pooh. The power of his images, which force onlookers to confront the fact that the essence of war is death, has angered some who prefer to keep war sanitized. Vandals defaced his son's gravestone.

"I don't speak," he says. "I show people war. I show them the caskets they are not allowed to see. If people don't see what war does, they don't feel it. If they don't feel it, they don't care."

Military recruiters, who often have offices in high schools, prey on young men like Alex, who was first approached when he was sixteen. They cater to their insecurities, their dreams, and their economic deprivation. They promise them what the larger society denies them. Those of Latino descent and from divorced families, as Alex was, are especially vulnerable. Alex's brother Brian was approached by the military, which suggested that if he enlisted, he could receive $60,000 in signing bonuses and more than $27,000 in payments for higher education. The proposed Development, Relief and Education for Alien Minors Act, or DREAM Act, was designed to give undocumented young people a chance at citizenship provided they attend college—not usually an option for poor, often poorly educated and undocumented Latino youths who are prohibited from receiving Pell Grants—for at least two years or enlist and serve in the military. The military helped author the pending act and lobbied for it.

Alex told Carlos in their last conversation there was heavy fighting in Najaf. Alex usually asked his father not to "forget" him, but now, increasingly in the final days of his life, another word was taking the place of *forget*. It was *forgive*. He felt his father should not forgive him for what he was doing in Iraq. He told his father, "Dad, I hope you are proud of what I'm doing. Don't forgive me, Dad." The sentence bewildered his father. "Oh my God . . . forgive you? . . . I love you, you're my son, very proud, you're my son."

"I thought, when he died, my God, he has killed somebody," Carlos says quietly as he readied for an anti-war march organized by Veterans for Peace. "He feels guilty. If he returned home his mind would be destroyed. His heart would be torn apart. It is not normal to kill. How can they do this? How can they take our children?"

X.

Wounds That Never Heal

I flew to Kansas City to see Tomas Young. Tomas was paralyzed in Iraq in 2004. He was receiving hospice care at his home. I knew him by reputation and the movie documentary *Body of War*. He was one of the first veterans to publicly oppose the war in Iraq. He fought as long and as hard as he could against the war that crippled him, until his physical deterioration caught up with him.

"I had been toying with the idea of suicide for a long time because I had become helpless," he told me in his small house on the Kansas City outskirts where he intended to die. "I couldn't dress myself. People have to help me with the most rudimentary of things. I decided I did not want to go through life like that anymore. The pain, the frustration. . . "

He stopped abruptly and called his wife. "Claudia, can I get some water?" She opened a bottle of water, took a swig so it would not spill when he sipped, and handed it to him.

"I felt at the end of my rope," the thirty-three-year-old Army veteran went on. "I made the decision to go on hospice care, to stop feeding and fade away. This way, instead of committing the conventional suicide and I am out of the picture, people have a way to stop by or call and say their goodbyes. I felt this was a fairer way to treat people than to just go out with a note. After the anoxic brain injury in 2008 [a complication that Young suffered] I lost a lot of dexterity and strength in my upper body. So, I wouldn't be able to shoot myself or even open the pill bottle to give myself an overdose. The only way I could think of doing it was to have Claudia open the pill bottle for me, but I didn't want her implicated."

"After you made that decision, how did you feel?" I asked.

"I felt relieved," he answered. "I finally saw an end to this four-and-a-half-year fight. If I were in the same condition I was in during the filming of *Body of War*, in a manual chair, able to feed and dress myself and transfer from my bed to the wheelchair, you and I would not be having this discussion. I can't even watch the movie anymore because it makes me sad to see how I was, compared to how I am. . . Viewing the deterioration, I decided it was best to go out now rather than regress more."

Young was crippled for a war that should never have been fought. He was crippled for the lies of politicians. He was crippled for war profiteers. He was crippled for the careers of generals. He bore all this upon his body. And there are hundreds of thousands of other broken bodies like his in Baghdad, Kandahar, Peshawar, the Walter Reed medical center, and hospitals in Russia and Ukraine. Mangled bodies and corpses, broken dreams, unending grief, betrayal, corporate profit, these are the true products of war. Tomas Young was the face of war they do not want you to see.

On April 4, 2004, Tomas was crammed into the back of a two-and-a-half-ton Army truck with twenty other soldiers in Sadr City, Iraq. Insurgents opened fire on the truck from above.

"It was like shooting ducks in a barrel," he said. A bullet from an AK-47 severed his spinal column. A second bullet shattered his knee. At first, he did not know he had been shot. He felt woozy. He tried to pick up his M16. He couldn't lift his rifle from the truck bed. That was when he knew something was terribly wrong.

"I tried to say, 'I'm going to be paralyzed, someone shoot me right now,' but there was only a hoarse whisper that came out because my lungs had collapsed," he said. "I knew the damage. I wanted to be taken out of my misery."

His squad leader, Staff Sgt. Robert Miltenberger, bent over and told him he would be all right. A few years later Tomas would see a clip of Miltenberger weeping as he recounted the story of how he had lied to Young.

"I tried to contact him," said Tomas, whose long red hair and flowing beard make him look like a biblical prophet. "I can't find him. I want to tell him it is OK."

Tomas had been in Iraq five days. It was his first deployment. After being wounded, he was sent to an Army hospital in Kuwait, and although his legs, now useless, lay straight in front of him, he felt as if he was still sitting cross-legged on the floor of the truck. That sensation lasted for about three weeks. It was an odd and painful initiation into his life as a paraplegic. His body, from then on, would play tricks on him. He was transferred from Kuwait to the U.S. military hospital at Landstuhl, Germany, and then to Walter Reed in Washington, D.C. He asked if he could meet Ralph Nader, and Nader visited him in the hospital with Phil Donahue. Donahue, who had been fired by MSNBC a year earlier for speaking out against the war, would go on, with Ellen Spiro, to make the 2007 film *Body of War*, an account of Tomas's daily struggle with his physical and emotional scars. In the documentary, he suffers dizzy spells that force him to lower his head into his hands. He wears frozen gel inserts in a cooling jacket because he cannot control his body temperature. He struggles to find a solution to his erectile dysfunction. He downs fistfuls of medications—carbamazepine, for nerve pain; coumadin, a blood thinner; tizanidine, an anti-spasm medication; gabapentin, another nerve pain medication; bupropion, an antidepressant; omeprazole, for morning nausea; and morphine. His mother must insert a catheter into his penis. He joins Cindy Sheehan, whose son was killed in Iraq, at Camp Casey in Crawford, Texas, to protest with Iraq Veterans Against the War. His first wife leaves him.

"You know, you see a guy who's paralyzed, and in a wheelchair, and you think he's just in a wheelchair," he says in *Body of War*. "You don't think about the, you know, the stuff inside that's paralyzed. I can't cough because my stomach muscles are paralyzed, so I can't work up the full coughing energy. I'm more susceptible to urinary tract infections, and there's a great big erection sidebar to this whole story."

In early March 2008 a blood clot in his right arm—the arm that bears a color tattoo of a character from Maurice Sendak's *Where the Wild Things Are*—caused his arm to swell. He was taken to the Kansas City Veterans Affairs hospital, where he was given the blood thinner coumadin before being released. One month later, the VA took him off coumadin, and soon afterward the clot migrated to one of his lungs. He suffered a massive pulmonary embolism and fell into a coma. When he awoke from the coma in the hospital he could barely speak. He had lost most of his upper-body mobility and short-term memory, and his speech was slurred.

It was then that he began to experience debilitating pain

in his abdomen. The hospital would not give him narcotics because the drugs would slow digestion, making it harder for the bowels to function. Tomas could digest only soup and Jell-O. In November, in a desperate bid to halt the pain, he had his colon removed. He was fitted with a colostomy bag. The pain disappeared for a few days and then came roaring back. He could not hold down food, even pureed food, because his stomach opening had shrunk. The doctors dilated his stomach. He could eat only soup and oatmeal. That was enough.

"I will go off the feeding [tube]," he said, "after me and my wife's anniversary," April 20, the date on which he married Claudia in 2012. "I was married once before. It didn't end well. It was a non-amicable divorce. At first, I thought I would [just] wait for my brother and his wife, my niece, and my grandparents to visit me, but the one thing I will miss most in my life is my wife. I want to spend a little more time with her. I want to spend a full year with someone without the problems that plagued my previous [marriage]. I don't know how long it will take when I stop eating. If it takes too long, I may take steps to quicken my departure. I have saved a bottle of liquid morphine. I can down that at one time with all my sleeping medication."

Tomas's room is painted a midnight blue and has a large cutout of Batman on one wall. He loved the superhero as a child, because "he was a regular person who had a horrible thing happen to him and wanted to save society."

Tomas joined the Army immediately after 9/11 to go to Afghanistan and hunt down the people behind the attacks. He did not oppose the Afghanistan war. "In fact, if I had been injured in Afghanistan, there would be no *Body of War* movie to begin with," he said. But he never understood the call to invade Iraq. "When the Japanese attacked Pearl Harbor, we didn't invade China just because they looked the same," he said.

He became increasingly depressed about his impending deployment to Iraq when he was in basic training at Fort Benning, Georgia. He asked the battalion doctor for antidepressants. The doctor said he had to meet first with the unit's chaplain, who told him, "I think you will be happier when you get over to Iraq and start killing Iraqis."

"I was dumbstruck by his response," Tomas said.

He had not decided what would be done with his ashes. He flirted with the idea of having them plowed into ground where marijuana would be planted but then wondered if anyone would want to smoke the crop. He knows there will be no clergy at the memorial service held after his death. "It will just be people reminiscing over my life," he said.

"I spend a lot of time sitting here in my bedroom, watching TV or sleeping," he said. "I have found—I don't know if it is the result of my decision or not—[it is] equally hard to be alone or to be around people. This includes my wife. I am rarely happy. Maybe it is because when I am alone all I have with me are my thoughts, and my mind is a very hazardous place to go. When I am around people I feel as if I have to put on a façade of being the happy little soldier."

He listened, when he was well enough, to audiobooks with Claudia. Among them have been Al Franken's satirical book *Lies and the Lying Liars Who Tell Them* and Michael Moore's *The Official Fahrenheit 9/11 Reader*. He was a voracious reader but can no longer turn the pages of a book. He found some solace in the French film *The Intouchables*, about a quadriplegic and his caregiver, and *The Sessions*, a film based on an essay by the paralyzed poet Mark O'Brien.

Tomas, when he was in a wheelchair, found that many people behaved as if he was mentally disabled, or not even there. When he was being fitted for a tuxedo for a friend's wedding the salesman turned to his mother and asked her in front of him whether he could wear the company's shoes.

"I look at the TV through the lens of his eyes and can see he is invisible," said Claudia, standing in the living room as her husband rested in the bedroom. An array of books on death, the afterlife, and dying is spread out around her. "No one is sick [on television]. No one is disabled. No one faces death. Dying in America is a very lonely business."

"If I had known then what I know now," Tomas said, "I would not have gone into the military. But I was twenty-two, working various menial jobs, waiting tables, [working] in the copy department of an OfficeMax. My life was going nowhere. September 11 happened. I saw us being attacked. I wanted to respond. I signed up two days later. I wanted to be a combat journalist. I thought the military would help me out of my financial rut. I thought I could use the GI Bill to go to school."

Tomas was not the first young man to be lured into war and then callously discarded. His story has been told many times. It is the story of Hector in *The Iliad*. It is the story of Joe Bonham, the protagonist in Dalton Trumbo's 1939 novel *Johnny Got His Gun*, whose arms, legs, and face are blown away by an artillery shell, leaving him trapped in the inert remains of his body.

Bonham ruminates in the novel:

> He was the future he was a perfect picture of the future and they were afraid to let anyone see what the future was like. Already they were looking ahead they were figuring the future and somewhere in the future they

saw war. To fight that war they would need men and if men saw the future they wouldn't fight. So they were masking the future they were keeping the future a soft quiet deadly secret. They knew that if all the little people all the little guys saw the future they would begin to ask questions. They would ask questions and they would find answers and they would say to the guys who wanted them to fight they would say you lying thieving sons-of-bitches we won't fight we won't be dead we will live we are the world we are the future and we will not let you butcher us no matter what you say no matter what speeches you make no matter what slogans you write.[46]

For Tomas, the war, the wound, the paralysis, the wheelchair, the anti-war demonstrations, the wife who left him and the one who didn't, the embolism, the loss of motor control, the slurred speech, the colostomy, the IV line for narcotics implanted in his chest, the open bedsores that expose his bones, the despair—the crushing despair—the decision to die, came down to a girl. Aleksus, his only niece. She would not remember her uncle. But he lay in his dimly lit room, painkillers flowing into his broken body, and thought of her. He did not know exactly when he would die. But it had to be before her second birthday, in June. He did not want to mar that day with his death.

He asked me to help him write a last letter to George W. Bush and the politicians and generals who sent him to war he planned to release in March 2013, the tenth anniversary of the start of the U.S.-led invasion of Iraq. He could not hold a pen. I took dictation. He planned to kill himself by cutting off his feeding tube. After issuing the letter, which was widely circulated and translated into several languages, Tomas changed his mind about committing suicide. He decided he wanted more time with his wife, Claudia. But he and Claudia knew he did not have long. The couple moved from Kansas City to Portland, Oregon, and then to Seattle, where Tomas died on November 10, 2014, at the age of thirty-four.

Over the last eight months of Tomas's life, Veterans Affairs reduced his pain medication, charging he had become an addict. It was a decision that thrust him into a wilderness of agony. Tomas's existence became a constant battle with the VA. He suffered excruciating "breakthrough pain." The VA was indifferent. It cut his thirty-day supply of pain medication to seven days. Young, when the pills did not arrive on time, might as well have been nailed to a cross. Claudia, in an exchange of several emails with me since Tomas's death, remembered hearing her husband on the phone one day pleading with a VA doctor and finally saying: "So you mean to tell me it is better for me to live in pain than die on pain medicine in this disabled state?" At night, she said, he would moan and cry out.

"It was a battle of wills," Claudia told me in an email. "We were losing. Our whole time in Portland was spent dealing with trying to get what we needed to be at home and comfortable and pain free. THAT'S ALL WE WANTED, TO BE HOME AND PAIN FREE, to enjoy whatever time we had left."

They left Portland for Seattle to be closer to a good spinal cord injury unit. Also, Washington was one of the states that had legalized marijuana, which Young used extensively.

"Last week I called because his breakthrough pain started happening throughout the day," Claudia wrote in an email. "I was using more and more of the morphine and lorazepam. I was running out of pills. He had a high tolerance for pain, but it was getting bad. I called to report to the doctor that it was getting bad fast. I would not have enough pills to bridge him to the appointment on the twenty-fourth. The doctor was unsympathetic. He gave me a condescending lecture about strict narcotics regulations. I said, 'But my husband is in pain, what do I do?'"

Tomas tried to take enough sleeping pills to sleep away the pain. But he was able to rest for a prolonged period only every few days. The pain and exhaustion began to tear apart his frail body. He was dispirited. He was visibly weaker. He felt humiliated.

"Maybe he got so exhausted by the enduring of it all that he took a last sleep and never came back," Claudia wrote. "My conclusion is that he died in pain from the exhaustion of having to endure it. Early morning Monday, when I thought he was sleeping, I heard a silence I had never heard before. I couldn't hear him breathing. I was scared, but I knew. The first thing I did was liberate him from all the tubes and bags on his body. I cut off the feeding tube. I took off the ostomy bags. I removed the Foley catheter. I cleaned his body. I played music. We smoked a last joint together. I smoked for him. I started making calls.

"The funeral home instructed me to call the police," she wrote. "They arrived and concluded that there were no issues, but because of his young age they had to refer this to the medical examiner. The medical examiner came. He made the determination that due to his age that they would have to perform an autopsy. I said, 'Hey look at his body don't you think he has been mutilated enough? Are [you] going to desecrate his body even further?' So, he was cut open some more."

The VA called her to ask for the autopsy report.

Tomas's final days, Claudia said, were often "hopeless and humiliating."

This was his Last Letter:

To: George W. Bush and Dick Cheney
From: Tomas Young

I write this letter on the 10th anniversary of the Iraq War
on behalf of my fellow Iraq War veterans. I write this letter
on behalf of the 4,488 soldiers and Marines who died in
Iraq. I write this letter on behalf of the hundreds of thousands of veterans who have been wounded and on behalf
of those whose wounds, physical and psychological, have
destroyed their lives. I am one of those gravely wounded.
I was paralyzed in an insurgent ambush in 2004 in Sadr
City. My life is coming to an end. I am living under hospice care. I write this letter on behalf of husbands and
wives who have lost spouses, on behalf of children who
have lost a parent, on behalf of the fathers and mothers
who have lost sons and daughters and on behalf of those
who care for the many thousands of my fellow veterans
who have brain injuries. I write this letter on behalf of
those veterans whose trauma and self-revulsion for what
they have witnessed, endured and done in Iraq have led
to suicide and on behalf of the active-duty soldiers and
Marines who commit, on average, a suicide a day. I write
this letter on behalf of the some 1 million Iraqi dead
and on behalf of the countless Iraqi wounded. I write
this letter on behalf of us all—the human detritus your
war has left behind, those who will spend their lives in
unending pain and grief.

I write this letter, my last letter, to you, Mr. Bush
and Mr. Cheney. I write not because I think you grasp

the terrible human and moral consequences of your lies, manipulation and thirst for wealth and power. I write this letter because, before my own death, I want to make it clear that I, and hundreds of thousands of my fellow veterans, along with millions of my fellow citizens, along with hundreds of millions more in Iraq and the Middle East, know fully who you are and what you have done. You may evade justice but in our eyes you are each guilty of egregious war crimes, of plunder and, finally, of murder, including the murder of thousands of young Americans—my fellow veterans—whose future you stole.

Your positions of authority, your millions of dollars of personal wealth, your public relations consultants, your privilege and your power cannot mask the hollowness of your character. You sent us to fight and die in Iraq after you, Mr. Cheney, dodged the draft in Vietnam, and you, Mr. Bush, went AWOL from your National Guard unit. Your cowardice and selfishness were established decades ago. You were not willing to risk yourselves for our nation but you sent hundreds of thousands of young men and women to be sacrificed in a senseless war with no more thought than it takes to put out the garbage.

I joined the Army two days after the 9/11 attacks. I joined the Army because our country had been attacked. I wanted to strike back at those who had killed some 3,000 of my fellow citizens. I did not join the Army to go to Iraq, a country that had no part in the September 2001 attacks and did not pose a threat to its neighbors, much less to the United States. I did not join the Army to "liberate" Iraqis or to shut down mythical weapons-of-mass-destruction facilities or to implant what you cynically called "democracy" in Baghdad and the Middle East. I did not join the Army to rebuild Iraq, which at the time you told us could be paid for by Iraq's oil revenues. Instead, this war has cost the United States over $3 trillion. I especially did not join the Army to carry out preemptive war. Preemptive war is illegal under international law. And as a soldier in Iraq I was, I now know, abetting your idiocy and your crimes. The Iraq War is the largest strategic blunder in U.S. history. It obliterated the balance of power in the Middle East. It installed a corrupt and brutal pro-Iranian government in Baghdad, one cemented in power through the use of torture, death squads and terror. And it has left Iran as the dominant force in the region. On every level—moral, strategic, military and economic—Iraq was a failure. And it was you, Mr. Bush and Mr. Cheney, who started this war. It is you who should pay the consequences.

I would not be writing this letter if I had been wounded fighting in Afghanistan against those forces that carried out the attacks of 9/11. Had I been wounded there I would still be miserable because of my physical deterioration and imminent death, but I would at least have the comfort of knowing that my injuries were a consequence of my own decision to defend the country I love. I would not have to lie in my bed, my body filled with painkillers, my life ebbing away, and deal with the fact that hundreds of thousands of human beings, including children, including myself, were sacrificed by you for little more than the greed of oil companies, for your alliance with the oil sheiks in Saudi Arabia, and your insane visions of empire.

I have, like many other disabled veterans, suffered from the inadequate and often inept care provided by the Veterans Administration. I have, like many other disabled veterans, come to realize that our mental and physical wounds are of no interest to you, perhaps of no interest to any politician. We were used. We were betrayed. And we have been abandoned. You, Mr. Bush, make much pretense of being a Christian. But isn't lying a sin? Isn't murder a sin? Aren't theft and selfish ambition sins? I am not a Christian. But I believe in the Christian ideal. I believe that what you do to the least of your brothers you finally do to yourself, to your own soul.

My day of reckoning is upon me. Yours will come. I hope you will be put on trial. But mostly I hope, for your sakes, that you find the moral courage to face what you have done to me and to many, many others who deserved to live. I hope that before your time on earth ends, as mine is now ending, you will find the strength of character to stand before the American public and the world, and in particular the Iraqi people, and beg for forgiveness.

XI

Shadows of War

In an instant, industrial warfare can kill dozens, even hundreds of people, who never see their attackers. The power of these industrial weapons is indiscriminate and staggering. They can take down apartment blocks in seconds, burying and crushing everyone inside. They can demolish villages and send tanks, planes, and ships up in fiery blasts. The wounds, for those who survive, leave terrible burns, blindness, amputation, and life-long pain and trauma.

In Peter van Agtmael's *2nd Tour Hope I Don't Die* and Lori Grinker's *Afterwar: Veterans from a World in Conflict*, two books of war photographs, we see pictures of war hidden from public view. These pictures are shadows, for only those who go to and suffer from war can fully confront the visceral horror of it, but they are at least an attempt to unmask war's savagery.

"Over ninety percent of this soldier's body was burned when a roadside bomb hit his vehicle, igniting the fuel tank and burning two other soldiers to death," reads the caption in van Agtmael's book next to a photograph of the bloodied body of a soldier in an operating room. "His camouflage uniform dangled over the bed, ripped open by the medics who had treated him on the helicopter. Clumps of his skin had peeled away, and what was left of it was translucent. He was in and out of consciousness, his eyes stabbing open for a few seconds. As he was lifted from the stretcher to the ER bed, he screamed 'Daddy, Daddy, Daddy, Daddy,' then 'Put me to sleep, please put me to sleep.' There was another photographer in the ER, and he leaned his camera over the heads of the medical staff to get an overhead shot. The soldier yelled, 'Get that fucking camera out of my face.' Those were his last words. I visited his grave one winter afternoon six months later," van Agtmael wrote, "and the scene of his death is never far from my thoughts."[47]

"There were three of us inside, and the jeep caught fire," Israeli soldier Yossi Arditi, quoted in Grinker's book, says of the moment when a Molotov cocktail exploded in his vehicle. "The fuel tank was full, and it was about to explode, my skin was hanging from my arms and face—but I didn't lose my head. I knew nobody could get inside to help me, that my only way out was through the fire to the doors. I wanted to take my gun, but I couldn't touch it because my hands were burning."

Arditi spent six months in the hospital. He had surgery every two or three months, about twenty operations, over the next three years.

"People who see me, see what war really does," he says.[48]

Filmic and photographic images of combat are shorn of the heart-pounding fear, awful stench, deafening noise, and exhaustion of the battlefield. Such images turn confusion and chaos, the chief element of combat, into an artful war narrative. They turn war into porn. Soldiers and Marines, especially those who have never seen war, buy cases of beer and watch movies like *Platoon*, movies meant to denounce war, and as they do so revel in the despicable power of weapons.

Chronicles of war, such as these two books, that eschew images and scenes of combat begin to capture war's reality. War's effects are what the state and the press, the handmaiden of the war makers, work hard to keep hidden. If we really saw war, what war does to young minds and bodies, it would be harder to embrace the myth of war. If we had to stand over the mangled corpses of the schoolchildren killed in Afghanistan or Ukraine and listen to the wails of their parents, the clichés about liberating the women of Afghanistan or bringing freedom to the Afghan or Ukrainian people would be obscene. Therefore, war is carefully sanitized. Television reports give us the visceral thrill of force and hide from us the effects of bullets, tank rounds, iron fragmentation bombs, and artillery rounds. We taste a bit of war's exhilaration, but are protected from seeing what war actually does, its smells, noises, confusion, and most of all its overpowering fear. . .

The wounded, the crippled, and the dead are, in this great charade, swiftly carted offstage. They are war's refuse. We do not see them. We do not hear them. They are doomed, like wandering spirits, to float around the edges of our consciousness, ignored, even reviled. The message they tell is too unpleasant for us to hear.

Saul Alfaro, who lost his legs in the war in El Salvador, speaks in Grinker's book about the first and final visit from his girlfriend as he lay in an army hospital bed. "She had been my girlfriend in the military and we had planned to be married," he says. "But when she saw me in the hospital—I don't know exactly what happened, but later they told me when she saw me, she began to cry. Afterwards, she ran away and never came back."[49]

The public manifestations of gratitude are reserved for veterans who dutifully read from the script handed to them by the state. The veterans trotted out for viewing are those who are compliant and palatable, those we can stand to look at without horror, those who are willing to go along with the lie that war is about patriotism and is the highest good. "Thank you for your service," we are supposed to say. They are used to perpetuate the heroic fiction. We are used to honor it.

Gary Zuspann, who lives in a special enclosed environment in his parents' home in Waco, Texas, suffering from Gulf War syndrome, speaks in Grinker's book of feeling like "a prisoner of war" even after the war had ended.

"Basically, they put me on the curb and said, okay, fend for yourself," he says in the book. "I was living in a fantasy world where I thought our government cared about us and they take care of their own. I believed it was in my contract, that if you're maimed or wounded during your service in war, you should be taken care of. Now I'm angry."[50]

I went back to Sarajevo after covering the war for the *New York Times* and found hundreds of cripples trapped in rooms in apartment blocks with no elevators and no wheelchairs. Most were young men, many without limbs, being cared for by their elderly parents, war heroes left to rot.

Despair and suicide grip survivors. More Vietnam veterans committed suicide after the war than were killed during it. The inhuman qualities drilled into soldiers and Marines in wartime defeat them in peacetime. This is what Homer taught us in *The Iliad*, the great book on war, and *The Odyssey*, the great book on the long journey to recovery by professional killers. Many never readjust. They cannot emotionally connect with wives, children, parents, or friends, retreating into personal hells of self-destructive numbness, anguish and rage.

"They program you to have no emotion—like if somebody sitting next to you gets killed you just have to carry on doing your job and shut off," Steve Annabell, a British veteran of the Falklands War, says to Grinker. "When you leave the service, when you come back from a situation like that, there's no button they can press to switch your emotions back on. So, you walk around like a zombie. They don't deprogram you. If you become a problem, they just sweep you under the carpet.

"To get you to join up they do all these advertisements—they show people skiing down mountains and doing great things—but they don't show you getting shot at and people with their legs blown off or burning to death," he says. "They don't show you what really happens. It's just bullshit. And they never prepare you for it. They can give you all the training in the world, but it's never the same as the real thing."[51]

Those with whom veterans have most in common when the war is over are often those they fought.

"Nobody comes back from war the same," says Horacio Javier Benitez, who fought the British in the Falklands and is quoted in Grinker's book. "The person, Horacio, who was sent to war, doesn't exist anymore. It's hard to be enthusiastic about normal life; too much seems inconsequential. You contend with craziness and depression.

"Many who served in the Malvinas," he says, using the Argentine name of the islands, "committed suicide, many of my friends."[52]

"I miss my family," reads a wall graffito captured in one of van Agtmael's photographs. "Please God forgive the lives I took and let my family be happy if I don't go home again."

Next to the plea someone has drawn an arrow toward the words and written in thick black marker: "Fag!!!"

XII.

War as Myth

When Peter Jackson's World War I film, *They Shall Not Grow Old*, which miraculously transforms grainy, choppy, black-and-white archival footage from the war into a modern 3D color extravaganza, begins, he bombards us with the clichés used to ennoble war. Veterans, over background music, say things like "I wouldn't have missed it," "I would go through it all over again because I enjoyed the service life," and "It made me a man." It must have taken some effort after the war to find the tiny minority of veterans willing to utter this rubbish. Military life is a form of servitude; prolonged exposure to combat leaves you broken, scarred for life by trauma, and often so numb you have difficulty connecting with others—and the last thing war does is make you a man.

Far more common was the experience of the actor Wilfrid Lawson, who was wounded in the war and as a result had a metal plate in his skull. He drank heavily to dull the incessant pain. In his memoir, *Inside Memory*, Timothy Findley, who acted with him, recalled that Lawson "always went to bed sodden and all night long he would be dragged from one nightmare to another—often yelling—more often screaming—very often struggling physically to free himself of impeding bed-clothes and threatening shapes in the shadows." He would pound the walls, shouting "Help! Help! Help!"

"The noise, my dear—and the people," Lawson muttered in anguish.[53]

David Lloyd George, wartime prime minister of Britain, in his memoirs used language like this to describe the conflict:

> [I]nexhaustible vanity that will never admit a mistake . . . individuals who would rather the million perish than that they as leaders should own—even to themselves—that they were blunderers . . . the notoriety attained by a narrow and stubborn egotism, unsurpassed among the records of disaster wrought by human complacency . . . a bad scheme badly handled . . . impossible orders issued by Generals who had no idea what the execution of their commands really meant . . . this insane enterprise . . . this muddy and muddle-headed venture . . .[54]

The British Imperial War Museum, which was behind the Jackson film, had no interest in portraying the reality of war. War may be savage, brutal, and hard, but it is also, according to the myth, ennobling, heroic, and selfless. You can believe this drivel only if you have never been in combat, which is what allows Jackson to modernize a cartoon version of war.

The poet Siegfried Sassoon, in "The Hero," captured the cynicism of war:

> *"Jack fell as he'd have wished," the mother said,*
> *And folded up the letter that she'd read.*

"The Colonel writes so nicely." Something broke
In the tired voice that quavered to a choke.
She half looked up. "We mothers are so proud
Of our dead soldiers." Then her face was bowed.

Quietly the brother Officer went out.
He'd told the poor old dear some gallant lies
That she would nourish all her days, no doubt.
For while he coughed and mumbled, her weak eyes
Had shone with gentle triumph, brimmed with joy,
Because he'd been so brave, her glorious boy.
He thought how "Jack," cold-footed, useless swine,

Had panicked down the trench that night the mine
Went up at Wicked Corner; how he'd tried
To get sent home; and how, at last, he died,
Blown to small bits. And no one seemed to care
Except that lonely woman with white hair.[55]

Our own generals and politicians, who nearly two decades ago launched the greatest strategic blunder in American history and wasted $7 trillion on quagmires in the Middle East, are no less egotistical and incompetent than Putin. The images of our wars are as carefully controlled and censored as the images from World War I. While the futility and human carnage of our current conflicts are rarely acknowledged in public, one might hope that we could confront the suicidal idiocy of World War I a century later.

Leon Wolff, in his book *In Flanders Fields: The 1917 Campaign*, wrote of World War I:

It had meant nothing, solved nothing, and proved

nothing; and in so doing had killed 8,538,315 men and variously wounded 21,219,452. Of 7,750,919 others taken prisoner or missing, well over a million were later presumed dead; thus the total deaths (not counting civilians) approach ten million. The moral and mental defects of the leaders of the human race had been demonstrated with some exactitude. One of them (Woodrow Wilson) later admitted that the war had been fought for business interests; another (David Lloyd George) had told a newspaperman: "If people really knew, the war would be stopped tomorrow, but of course they don't—and can't know. The correspondents don't write and the censorship wouldn't pass the truth."[56]

There is no mention in Jackson's film of the colossal stupidity of the British general staff that sent hundreds of thousands of working-class Englishmen—they are seen grinning into the camera with their decayed teeth—in wave after wave, week after week, month after month, into the mouths of German machine guns to be killed or wounded. There is no serious exploration of the iron censorship that hid the realities of the war from the public and saw the press become a shill for warmongers. There is no investigation into how the war was used by the state, as it is today, as an excuse to eradicate civil liberties. There is no look at the immense wealth made by the arms manufacturers and contractors or how the war plunged Britain deep into debt with war-related costs totaling 70 percent of the gross national product. Yes, we see some pictures of gruesome wounds, digitally converted into color, yes, we hear how rats ate corpses, but the war in the film is carefully choreographed, stripped of the deafening sounds, repugnant smells, and most importantly the crippling fear and terror that make a battlefield a stygian nightmare. We glimpse dead bodies, but there are no long camera shots of the slow agony of those dying of horrific wounds. Sanitized images like these are war pornography. That they are no longer jerky and grainy and have been colorized in 3D merely gives old war porn a modern sheen.

"When the war was not very active, it was really rather fun to be in the front line," a veteran says in the film. "It was a sort of outdoor camp holiday with a slight spice of danger to make it interesting."

Insipid comments like that defined the perception of the war at home. The clash between a civilian population that saw the war as "a sort of outdoor camp holiday" and those who experienced it led to profound estrangement. The poet Charles Sorley wrote: "I should like so much to kill whoever was primarily responsible for the war."[57] And journalist and author Philip Gibbs noted that soldiers had a deep hatred of civilians who believed the lies. "They hated the smiling women in the streets. They loathed the old men. . . . They desired that profiteers should die by poison-gas. They prayed to God to get the Germans to send Zeppelins to England—to make the people know what war meant."[58]

There is no such thing as getting used to combat. Everyone in combat eventually reaches a breaking point, from the most sensitive and the most cowardly to the hardest combat veteran. Combat is a form of psychological and physical torture. Once you break down, as I did in the last war I covered in Kosovo, all appeals to duty, honor, patriotism, and manliness are useless.

Military studies have determined that after sixty days of continuous combat, 98 percent of those who survive will have become psychiatric casualties. The common trait among the 2 percent who were able to endure sustained combat was a pre-disposition toward "aggressive psychopathic personalities." Lt. Col. David Grossman wrote: "It is not too far from the mark to observe that there is something about continuous, inescapable combat which will drive 98 percent of all men insane, and the other 2 percent were crazy when they got there."[59]

The military cliques in American society are as omnipotent as they were in World War I. The symbols of war and militarism, then and now, have a quasi-religious aura. Our incompetent generals—such as David Petraeus, whose surges only prolonged the Iraq War and raised the casualty figures and whose idea to arm "moderate" rebels in Syria was a debacle—are as lionized as the pig-headed and vainglorious Gen. Douglas Haig, the British commander in chief. Haig, in a war where the defense was mechanized and attacks were not, resisted innovations such as the tank, the airplane, and the machine gun, which he called "a much-overrated weapon." He believed the cavalry would play the decisive role in winning the war. Haig, in the Battle of the Somme, oversaw 60,000 casualties on the first day of the offensive, July 1, 1916. None of his military objectives were achieved. Twenty thousand lay dead between the lines. The wounded cried out for days. This did not dampen Haig's ardor to sacrifice his soldiers. Determined to complete his plan of bursting through the German lines and unleashing his three divisions of cavalry on the fleeing enemy, he kept the waves of assaults going for four months until winter forced him to cease. By the time Haig was done, the Army had suffered more than 400,000 casualties and accomplished nothing. Lt. Col. E. T. F. Sandys, who saw five hundred of his soldiers killed or wounded on the first day at the Somme, wrote two months later, "I have never had a moment's peace since July 1st." He then shot himself to death in a London hotel room. Joe Sacco's illustrated book *The Great War*, a twenty-four-foot-long wordless panorama that depicts the first day of the Battle of Somme, ending with massive burial details, reveals far more truth about the horror of war than Jackson's elaborate restoration of old film.

The military historian B. H. Liddell Hart, who was gassed at the Somme, wrote in his diary, "He [Haig] was a man of supreme egoism and utter lack of scruple—who, to his overweening ambition, sacrificed hundreds of thousands of men. A man who betrayed even his most devoted assistants as well as the government which he served. A man who gained his ends by trickery of a kind that was not merely immoral but criminal."[60]

The American attorney Harold Shapiro, following World War I, examined the medical records of the Army on behalf of a disabled veteran. He was appalled at the reality these records elucidated and the misperception of the war within the public. The medical descriptions, he wrote, rendered "all that I had read and heard previously as being either fiction, isolated reminiscence, vague generalization or deliberate propaganda."[61] He published a book in 1937 titled *What Every Young Man Should Know about War*. It was pulled from circulation when the United States entered World War II and never reissued. It was the model for my book *What Every Person Should Know about War*, which also drew on medical, psychological, and military studies of the effects of combat.

Shapiro wrote in his chapter "Mental Reactions":

Q: What may happen to me after I bayonet my enemy in the face?
You may develop an hysterical tic—quick, sudden, convulsive spasms of twitching of your own facial muscles.

Q: What may happen to me after I bayonet my enemy in the abdomen?
You may be seized with abdominal contractions.

Q: What may happen to me following particularly horrible sights?
You may be seized with hysterical blindness.

Q: What may happen to me if I find the cries of the wounded unbearable?
You may develop hysterical deafness.

Q: What may happen to me should I be detailed to burial parties?
You may develop anosmia (loss of your sense of smell).[62]

In researching my book *What Every Person Should Know about War* I found a passage from the Office of the Surgeon General's *Textbook of Military Medicine* about how to manage troops that have been exposed to fatal doses of nuclear radiation. It read:

Fatally irradiated soldiers should receive every possible palliative treatment, including narcotics, to prolong their utility and alleviate their physical and psychological distress. Depending on the amount of fatal radiation, such soldiers may have several weeks to live and to devote to the cause. Commanders and medical personnel should be familiar with estimating survival time based on the onset of vomiting. Physicians should be prepared to give medications to alleviate diarrhea, and to prevent infection and other sequelae of radiation sickness in order to allow the soldier to serve as long as possible. The soldier must be allowed to make the full contribution to the war effort. He will already have made the ultimate sacrifice. He deserves a chance to strike back, and to do so while experiencing as little discomfort as possible.[63]

The German pacifist Ernst Friedrich collected two hundred photographs of gruesome wounds, piles of corpses in mass graves, the hangings and executions of deserters—their families were told they had "died of wounds"—and battlefield atrocities censored from the public in his 1924 book, *War Against War!* He juxtaposed the images against the propaganda that romanticized the conflict. His twenty-four close-ups of soldiers with grotesquely disfiguring facial wounds remain difficult to view. Friedrich was arrested when the Nazis came to power in 1933, his book was banned, and his Anti-War Museum closed. Beside a picture in his book of a nearly naked soldier dead in a trench, the text reads: "Mothers! This was the fate of your sons in the war; first murdered, then robbed to the skin and then left as grub for animals."[64]

Honestly examining past wars gives us the ability to understand current wars. But this is a Herculean struggle. The public is fed, and yearns for, the myth. It is empowering and ennobling. It celebrates supposed national virtues and military prowess. It allows an alienated population to feel part of a national collective engaged in a noble crusade. The celebration of the destructive force of our weaponry makes us feel personally empowered. All wars, past and present, are effectively shrouded in this myth. Those who decried the waste and carnage during World War I, such as Keir Hardie, the head of the Independent Labour Party, were jeered in the streets. Adam Hochschild's book *To End All Wars: A Story of Loyalty and Rebellion, 1914–1918* details the struggle by pacifists and a handful of journalists and dissidents during the war to make the truth known, who were mocked, silenced, and often jailed.

"Few of us can hold on to our real selves long enough to discover the momentous truths about ourselves and this whirling earth to which we cling," wrote J. Glenn Gray, a combat veteran of World War II, in *The Warriors: Reflections on Men in Battle*. "This is especially true of men in war. The great god Mars tries to blind us when we enter his realm, and when we leave, he gives us a generous cup of the waters of Lethe to drink."[65]

Jackson closes the film with an army ditty about prostitution. "You might forget the gas and shell," the song goes, "but you'll nev'r forget the Mademoiselle! Hinky-dinky, parlez-vous?"

Tens of thousands of girls and women, whose brothers, fathers, sons, and husbands were dead or crippled, and whose homes often had been destroyed, became impoverished and often homeless. They were easy prey for the brothels, including the military-run brothels, and the pimps that serviced the soldiers. There is nothing amusing or cute about lying on a straw mat and being raped by as many as sixty men a day, unless you are the rapist.

It is fortunate all the participants in the war are dead. They would find the film another example of the monstrous lie that denied their reality, ignored or minimized their suffering, and never held the militarists, careerists, profiteers, and imbeciles who prosecuted the war accountable. War is the raison d'être of technological society. It unleashes demons. And those who profit from these demons, then and now, work hard to keep them hidden.

XIII.

War Memorials

War memorials and museums are temples to the god of war. The hushed voices, the well-tended grass, the flapping of the flags allow us to ignore how and why our young died. They hide the futility and waste of war. They sanitize the savage instruments of death that turn young soldiers and Marines into killers, and small villages in Vietnam or Afghanistan or Iraq into hellish bonfires. There are no images in these memorials of men or women with their guts hanging out of their bellies, screaming pathetically for their mothers. We do not see mangled corpses being shoved in body bags. There are no sights of children burned beyond recognition or moaning in horrible pain. There are no blind and deformed wrecks of human beings limping through life.

War memorials and museums, war movies and books, provide the mental images and distorted historical references to justify new wars. We are forever saving Private Ryan. We view ourselves as eternal liberators. These plastic representations of war reconfigure the past in light of the present. War memorials and romantic depictions of war in films are the social and moral props used to create the psychological conditions to wage new wars.

War memorials are quiet, still, reverential, and tasteful. And, like church, such sanctuaries are important, but they allow us to forget that these men and women were used and often betrayed by those who led the nation into war. The memorials do not tell us that some always grow rich from large-scale human suffering. They do not explain that politicians play the great games of world power and stoke fear for their own advancement. They forget that young men and women in uniform are pawns in the hands of cynics. They mask the ignorance, raw ambition, and greed of the masters of war.

There is a yearning, one seen in the collective memory that has grown up around World War II and the Holocaust, to turn the industrial slaughter into a tribute to the triumph of the human spirit. The reality is too unpalatable. The human need to make sense of slaughter, to give it a grandeur it does not possess.

Primo Levi, who survived Auschwitz, fought against the mendacity of collective memory until his suicide. He railed against distorting the Holocaust and the war by giving it a false, moral narrative. He wrote that the contemporary history of the Third Reich could be "reread as a war against memory, an Orwellian falsification of memory, falsification of reality, negation of reality."[66] He wondered if "we who have returned" have "been able to understand and make others understand our experience?"[67] He wrote, referring to the Jewish collaborator Chaim Rumkowski, who ran the Lodz ghetto on behalf of the Nazis, that "we are all mirrored in Rumkowski, his ambiguity is ours, it is our second nature, we hybrids molded from clay and spirit. His fever is ours, the fever of Western civilization that 'descends into hell with trumpets and drums,' and its miserable adornments are the distorting image of our symbols of social prestige." We, like Rumkowski, "come to terms with power, forgetting that we are all in the ghetto, that the ghetto is walled in, that outside the ghetto reign the lords of death, and that close by the train is waiting."[68]

A war memorial that attempted to depict the reality of war would be too subversive. It would condemn us and our capacity for evil. It would show that human beings, when the restraints are cut, are intoxicated by mass killing. It would tell us that the celebration of national greatness is the celebration of our technological capacity to kill. It would warn us that war is always morally depraved, that even in "good" wars such as World War II, all can become war criminals. We dropped the atomic bomb on Hiroshima and Nagasaki. But this narrative of war is unsettling. It does not create a collective memory that serves the interests of those who wage war. It does not permit us to wallow in self-exaltation. There are times—World War II and the Serb assault on Bosnia would be examples—when a population is pushed into a war. There are times when a nation must ingest the poison of violence to survive. But this violence always deforms and maims those who use it.

The detritus of war, the old cannons and artillery pieces rolled out to stand near memorials, were curious and alluring objects in my childhood. But these displays angered my father, a Presbyterian minister who was in North Africa as an Army sergeant during World War II. The lifeless, clean, and neat displays of weapons and puppets in uniforms were being used, he said, to purge the reality of war. These memorials sanctified violence. They turned the instruments of violence—the tanks, machine guns, rifles, and airplanes—into an aesthetic of death.

These memorials dignify slaughter. They prepare the nation for the next inferno. The myth of war manufactures a collective memory that ennobles the war. The intimate, personal experience of violence, which few want to hear, turns those who return from war into internal exiles.

I went to one of the massive temples across the country where we celebrate our state religion. The temple I visited was Boston's Fenway Park. The Fourth of July worship service that I attended—a game between the Red Sox and the Baltimore Orioles—was a day late because of a rescheduling caused by Tropical Storm Arthur. When the crowd sang "The Star-Spangled Banner," a gargantuan American flag descended to cover the "Green Monster," the over thirty-seven-foot-high wall in left field. Patriotic music blasted from loudspeakers. Col. Lester A. Weilacher, commander of the 66th Air Base Group at Massachusetts' Hanscom Air Force Base, wearing a light blue short-sleeved Air Force shirt and dark blue pants, threw the ceremonial first pitch. A line of Air Force personnel stood along the left field wall. The fighter jets—our angels of death—that usually roar over the stadium on the Fourth were absent. But the face of Fernard Frechette, a ninety-three-year-old World War II veteran who was attending, appeared on the thirty-eight-by-one-hundred-foot Jumbotron above the center-field seats as part of Fenway's "Hats Off to Heroes" program, which honors military veterans or active-duty members at every game. The crowd stood and applauded. Army National Guard Sgt. Ben Arnold had been honored at the previous game, on Wednesday. Arnold said his favorite Red Sox player was Mike Napoli. Arnold, who fought in Afghanistan, makes about $27,000 a year. Napoli makes $16 million. The owners of the Red Sox clear about $60 million annually.

The religious reverence—repeated in sports arenas throughout the United States—is used to justify our bloated war budget and endless wars. Schools and libraries are closing. Unemployment and underemployment are chronic. Our infrastructure is broken and decrepit. We wasted $7 trillion on the wars in the Middle East. But the military remains as unassailable as Jesus, or, among those who have season tickets at Fenway Park, the Red Sox. The military is the repository of patriotism. No public official dares criticize the armed forces or challenge their divine right to more than half of all the nation's discretionary spending. And although we may be distrustful of government, the military—in the twisted logic of the American mind—is somehow separate.

The heroes of war and the heroes of sport are indistinguishable in militarized societies. War is sold to a gullible public as a noble game. Few have the athletic prowess to play professional sports, but almost any young man or woman can go to a recruiter and sign up to be a military hero. The fusion of the military with baseball, along with the recruitment ads that appeared intermittently on the television screens mounted on green iron pillars throughout Fenway Park, catered to this illusion: *Sign up. You will be part of a professional team. We will show you in your uniform on the Jumbotron in Fenway Park. You will be a hero like Mike Napoli.*

The crowd of some 37,000, which paid on average about $70 for a ticket, dutifully sang hosannas—including "God Bless America" in the seventh inning—to the flag and the instruments of death and war. It blessed and applauded a military machine that, ironically, oversees the wholesale surveillance of everyone in the ballpark and has the power under the National Defense Authorization Act to snatch anyone in the stands and hold him or her indefinitely in a military facility. There was no mention of targeted assassinations of U.S. citizens, kill lists, or those lost or crippled in the wars. The crowd roared its approval every time the military was mentioned.

War is not a sport. It is about killing. It is dirty, messy, and deeply demoralizing. The pay is lousy. The working conditions are horrific. And those who come back from war are usually discarded. The veterans who died waiting for medical care from Veterans Affairs hospitals could, if they were alive, explain the difference between being a multimillion-dollar-a-year baseball star and a lance corporal home from Iraq or Afghanistan.

All religions need relics. Old uniforms, bats, balls, gloves, and caps are preserved in the Baseball Hall of Fame, like the bones of saints in churches. In that Cooperstown, New York, museum you walk by glass cases of baseball relics on your way to the third-floor display bearing the words "Sacred Ground: Examining ballparks of the past and present, this exhibit takes a look at America's cathedrals of the game." At ballparks the teams display statues of their titans—there is one of left fielder Ted Williams outside Fenway Park. And tens of thousands of dollars are paid for objects used by the immortals. A 1968 Mickey Mantle jersey sold on auction for $201,450. Team minutiae and statistics are preserved, much as monasteries preserve details of the lives and deaths of saints. Epic tales of glory and defeat are etched into the permanent record. The military has astutely deified itself through the fans' deification of teams.

The collective euphoria experienced in stadiums gives to many anxious Americans what they crave. They flock to the temples of sport while most places of traditional religious worship in the United States are largely deserted on the Sabbath. Those packed into the stadiums feel as if they and everyone around them speak the same language. They believe those in the crowd are one entity. And they all hate the same enemy.

To walk through Fenway Park in a New York Yankees shirt is to court verbal abuse. To be identified as a Yankees fan after a game in one of the bars outside the park is unwise. The longing to belong, especially in a society where many have lost their sense of place and identity, is skillfully catered to by both the professional sports and the military machine. Many sports devotees return after the games to dead-end jobs, or no jobs, to massive personal debt, to the bleakness of the future. No wonder supplicants at Fenway Park part with such large sums of money to be entranced by fantasy for a few hours. And no wonder it is hard to distinguish the fantasy of a game from the fantasy of the military. Life in the Army or the Marines begins to look like spending a few years at Fenway. And that is why the military invests so much in sponsoring sporting events. Between innings that Saturday, the screen above my head flashed segments called "U.S. Army Presents Top Prospects" that showcased promising ballplayers. Recruitment ads appeared at intervals. And the logo "Discover a Stronger Future. There's Strong. There's Army Strong" was ubiquitous. The Pentagon spends some $5 billion a year on recruiting, advertising, public affairs, and psychological operations. And much of that is targeted at the audiences of professional sports.

The owners of coal companies at the turn of the twentieth century in southern West Virginia found that by funding local baseball teams they could blunt the solidarity of workers. Towns and coal camps rallied around their individual teams. Workers divided themselves according to team loyalty. Sport rivalries became personal. The owners, elated, used the teams to help fracture the labor movement. And the infernal logic is no different today. The players on a baseball team—who usually do not come from the city they represent—are used to promote a provincial chauvinism and a false sense of belonging and empowerment. And the financial, emotional, and intellectual energy invested by fans in these well-choreographed spectacles keeps the onlookers docile and supine.

The *Boston Globe* and the Knight Ridder media chain reported in 2005 that Phillip H. Morse, a minority partner of the Boston Red Sox, chartered his private jet to the Central Intelligence Agency, which used it to pick up terrorism suspects in the Middle East and Europe and fly them to Guantánamo Bay. The plane was spotted in Cairo on February 18, 2003, according to Knight Ridder. The imam of Milan, Hassan Mustafa Osama Nasr, also known as Abu Omar, had been kidnapped the day before on a Milan street by the CIA and Italy's Military Intelligence and Security Service. He was then flown clandestinely to Egypt. It is nearly certain that Morse's plane was used for that flight. The imam was allegedly beaten and tortured in an Egyptian-run "black site." The Gulfstream jet, the *Globe* reported, rented for $5,365 an hour, which, it calculated, worked out to $128,760 for a twenty-four-hour day, or about $900,000 a week. Not even the highest-paid star on the Red Sox makes that much money.

The use of the Morse jet to carry out extraordinary rendition exposes the dark side of professional sports, how it is used by oligarchs and the military to manipulate and control us. The Red Sox logo that normally adorns the plane was missing. But the logo in any case would not have been visible to the imam, whose head would have been covered with a hood. The only difference between the imam and the rest of us is that we don't require blindfolds.

XIV.

The Golden Age of Heroes

I am descended from one of three brothers who fought at Gettysburg in July 1863. Clark S. Edwards was a Union general. Albert M. Edwards was a colonel in the elite Iron Brigade. Congress voted in 2018 to award him a posthumous Medal of Honor. David A. Edwards is my great-great-grandfather. He was a sergeant in the 5th Maine, and his war diaries, letters, brass cartridge box plate, and pocket watch are next to me as I write.

More than 50,000 soldiers were killed, wounded, or reported missing here in July 1863, many of them dying in terrible agony on the battlefield or carted off to improvised hospitals where arms and legs were swiftly amputated and tossed into large heaps on the floor. Abysmal hygiene—surgeons would nonchalantly wipe the blood from their bone saws on their pus-stained smocks and move on to the next victim—caused infection, blood poisoning, and gangrene. To buy time, regiments such as the 1st Minnesota were ordered into battle against superior forces and as a result were decimated within minutes. Hundreds of African American men, women, and children, many born free in the surrounding Pennsylvania towns, were abducted by invading Confederate forces led by Gen. Robert E. Lee and shipped south to be sold in the slave markets in Richmond, Virginia. Confederate and at times Union forces looted homes, farms, and shops. For three days in the summer of 1863, there was an orgy of destruction, death, and suffering on this ground.

An estimated 750,000 soldiers were killed by combat, accident, starvation, and disease in the Civil War, more than the U.S. dead of World War I and World War II combined. Rifled muskets and rifled artillery vastly increased the range and accuracy of fire over the eighteenth century's smoothbore muskets and cannons, but the advance in weaponry did nothing to perturb the generals who clung to outdated and suicidal tactics. They sent their soldiers marching forward in parade-ground lines into murderous volleys as if they were on a Napoleonic battlefield. The inability of most generals to adapt, as Allen C. Guelzo wrote in *Gettysburg: The Last Invasion*, "makes the Civil War look like an exercise in raw stupidity equivalent to the slaughters on the Western Front [of World War I]."[69]

The brothers were from Bethel, Maine. David was wounded in his right arm in 1864, days after the Battle of the Wilderness in northeast Virginia. As he walked back from the front lines looking for a field hospital, he saw what had become a depressingly familiar sight, wounded men screaming and writhing in agony amid the dead. He would be haunted as much by the aftermath of Civil War battles as by the fighting itself.

"Cold and rainy," David wrote in his diary on May 12, 1864. "2nd Corps captured a rebel division of infantry, 3 major generals, took their works, 25 guns. Our division sent to support them. We made a charge on pits. I received a wound in the right arm. Went to the rear."

Four days later, on May 16, he wrote: "Still in Fredericks-
burg, nothing to eat, no care, nothing that we need."

As a boy I hiked to the top of Monument Hill in Leeds,
Maine. On the summit is a thirty-foot-high granite obelisk
erected by the Union general and fierce abolitionist Oliver
Otis Howard, who was from Leeds. He lost his right arm in
the Battle of Fair Oaks/Seven Pines in a June 1862 action for
which he was awarded the Medal of Honor. After the war he
was the commissioner of the Freedmen's Bureau and helped
found historically black Howard University in Washington,
D.C., serving as the school's president from 1869 to 1874.
He called his obelisk a peace monument and inscribed on it:
"Peace Was Sure 1865." Howard railed against the glorification
of war, writing, "We cannot well exaggerate . . . the horrors, the
hateful ravages, and the countless expense of war." Stories of
war, he said, should serve only one purpose, to "show plainly to
our children that war, with its embodied woes and furies, must
be avoided."[70]

By focusing on battlefield exploits we too often blot out the
suffering of the soldiers, the families that lost sons, brothers,
and husbands, and the hundreds of thousands of children left
without fathers. We ignore the crippling physical and psychological wounds that plague veterans. Units in the Civil War
were raised locally. Towns and villages could within one day
of heavy fighting lose a third or more of their men, plunging
entire populations into collective grief. Maine, per capita, sent
more men to war than any other Northern state. There is hardly
a town in Maine that does not have a Civil War memorial with
a shockingly long list of names. The weight of the loss was
still felt when I was a boy in the 1960s, especially, in my case,
because my grandmother lived with her grandfather, David,

the onetime sergeant, until he died when she was eight. He was wracked by pain from his wound until the end of his life.

Thomas D. Marbaker, the author of *History of the Eleventh New Jersey Volunteers: From Its Organization to Appomattox* wrote of the aftermath of the battle:

> Burial Parties were sent out, and those who could get away from their commands went out to view the scene of carnage, and surely it was a scene never to be forgotten. Upon the open fields, like sheaves bound by the reaper, in crevices of the rocks, behind fences, trees and buildings; in thickets, where they had crept for safety only to die in agony; by stream or wall or hedge, wherever the battle had raged or their waking steps could carry them, lay the dead. Some with faces bloated and blackened beyond recognition, lay with glassy eyes staring up at the blazing summer sun; others, with faces downward and clenched hands filled with grass or earth, which told of the agony of the last moments. Here a headless trunk, there a severed limb; in all the grotesque positions that unbearable pain and intense suffering contorts the human form, they lay. Upon the faces of some death had frozen a smile; some showed the trembling shadow of fear, while upon others was indelibly set the grim stamp of determination. All around was the wreck the battle-storm leaves in its wake—broken caissons, dismounted guns, small arms bent and twisted by the storm or dropped and scattered by disabled hands; dead and bloated horses, torn and ragged equipment, and all the sorrowful wreck that the waves of battle leave at their ebb; and overall, hugging

the earth like a fog, poisoning every breath, the pestilential stench of decaying humanity.[71]

The miasma of rotting bodies after the Battle of Gettysburg, exacerbated by the carcasses of 5,000 horses and mules, lingered for weeks. Residents in the town of Gettysburg had to cover their mouths and noses when they went outside.

"A sickening, overpowering, awful stench announced the presence of the unburied dead upon which the July sun was mercilessly shining and at every step the air grew heavier and fouler until it seemed to possess a palpable horrible density that could be seen and felt and cut with a knife . . . ," wrote Cornelia Hancock, a Union nurse at Gettysburg.[72]

Time has long since erased these gruesome sights and smells from the battlefield national park, along with the disorienting confusion, fear, and deafening noise of combat. The groomed fields and undulating hills are dotted with stately monuments to Civil War units and leaders. The park memorializes the aspect of the battle and the war the state wants us to memorialize. It tells us that patriotism comes from serving the state, although, as Ulysses S. Grant said, the Confederate cause was "one of the worst for which a people ever fought."

The Gettysburg Park implicitly celebrates nationalism and elevates the warrior caste. The Confederates, fighting to preserve slavery, have, with the deified Lee, been admitted into our pantheon of national heroes because of their martial valor. The cruelty and folly of war, along with the holocaust of slavery and the widespread grief and suffering caused by the staggering numbers of dead and wounded, are treated as tangential aspects eclipsed by the great sacrifice.

I stood on Little Round Top, a hill within the park where the breastworks erected by the 5th Maine are still visible. David, who fought there, had little use for senior officers, including his brother the general, who, like many other generals, callously sent men to be slaughtered to burnish battlefield credentials. In a letter to his wife dated August 16, 1864, from the hospital at Camp Fry in Illinois he calls his brother "a miserable, lying scoundrel" who is "devoid of any moral or manly principle or honor," adding: "His nature is composed of selfishness and egoism."

Clark Edwards, a friend of Gen. Joshua Chamberlain, like Chamberlain and the New York politician and general Dan Sickles, spent the postwar years elevating himself as an icon of battlefield heroism and used that image to further his political ambitions, which included an unsuccessful run for governor of Maine as the Democratic nominee. (Guelzo wrote of Sickles, whose military incompetence nearly led to a Union defeat, that he "oozed sleaze and dissimulation from every pore.")

David Edwards, along with the other soldiers on Little Round Top, was acutely aware that Chamberlain's 20th Maine played only a secondary role in repulsing the Confederates. The Confederates were denied Little Round Top, an important piece of raised topography on the battlefield, because of the foresight of Gen. Gouverneur K. Warren and the alacrity and courage of brigade commander Gen. Strong Vincent and Col. Patrick O'Rorke, who commanded the 140th New York Infantry. But because Vincent and O'Rorke were killed in the defense of the hill, there was little impediment to Chamberlain's tireless revisionist accounts of the fight. Chamberlain, in addition to being awarded, like Sickles, the Medal of Honor, became the president of Bowdoin College and served four terms as the governor of Maine. He authored "seven accounts of Gettysburg," Guelzo wrote, "giving himself the starring role on Little Round Top, and Little Round Top the starring role in the battle." Guelzo adds: "Mortality, and the ex-professor's considerable flair for self-promotion, vaulted him ahead of others."[73]

It was the third brother, Albert, who would be at the center of some of the most savage fighting at Gettysburg, narrowly escaping death. He was at the time a captain in the 24th Michigan, one of five regiments in the Iron Brigade. He had attended the University of Michigan and been a newspaper reporter, an experience that helped make his official battlefield reports literate and at times moving.

The Iron Brigade was one of the most celebrated brigades in the Union Army, easily identifiable by the black "Hardee hats" its members wore instead of the blue caps typical of most Union troops. By the end of the war, it would lead all federal brigades in percentage of deaths in battle. But the combat-forged hardness of its troops came with a cost.

My grandmother had the 1891 edition of *History of 24th Michigan of the Iron Brigade*, which I now possess. It has a dried rose between pages 234 and 235. I was haunted when I first read it as a boy, not only by the horrific losses endured by the 24th Michigan in the first day of the battle, which left Albert in command, but by the execution of a deserter, Pvt. John P. Woods of the 19th Indiana, on June 12 on the way north.

"At about 2 o'clock the Iron Brigade led the column into a field, preceded by the prisoner sitting on his coffin," Sgt. Sullivan D. Green wrote in the history. "In silence, three sides of a hollow square were formed. The coffin was placed on the ground, the prisoner alighted from the ambulance with the chaplain who held a few moments' converse with the doomed man. . . "[74]

Twelve soldiers were selected for the firing squad and issued muskets. One of the muskets had a blank.

"A handkerchief was placed over his eyes, and his arms and legs were bound," Green wrote. "At the command 'attention,' the usual word of caution or preparation, they were to fire. The hat [in the hand of an officer] was lifted—10,000 eyes were strained in one breathless gaze—it was lowered, and many eyes withdrew from the sight that was to follow. The report of arms was heard, and a lifeless body fell backward to the dust!"[75]

Woods's wife was seriously ill. He had tried to go home to be with her.

On the first day of the Battle of Gettysburg, the Iron Brigade, heavily outnumbered by Confederates, attempted to hold the Union line at McPherson's Ridge. By nightfall only 99 of the 496 members of the 24th Michigan had not been killed, wounded, or captured, a loss of 80 percent. Albert and two lieutenants were the only officers remaining on the field. The entire brigade had been mauled, reduced to 600 soldiers from the original 1,885. The survivors were repositioned on Culp's Hill.

I stood on McPherson's Ridge, the scene of the bloodbath 156 years ago that took the life of Maj. Gen. John F. Reynolds. The shade of the towering trees and slight rustle of the leaves gave this isolated part of the battlefield a gentle tranquility. But by the end of July 1, 1863, the ground surrounding me was covered with Union dead and wounded, many of whom had to be abandoned in the slow retreat toward town.

"Coming up in the wake of the attack he heard 'dreadful howls' in the woods on the ridge, and when he went over to investigate, he found that the source of the racket was the wounded of both sides," Shelby Foote, writing in *Stars in Their*

Courses: The Gettysburg Campaign, June–July 1863, said of Confederate Gen. William Dorsey Pender, who would be mortally wounded the next day. "Several were foaming at the mouth, as though mad, and seemed not even to be aware they were screaming."[76]

My grandmother began her life in the shadow of one war—the Civil War—and her life ended in the shadow of another—World War II. Her only son, my uncle Maurice, had fought as an Army infantryman in the South Pacific in World War II, where he was wounded by a mortar blast. He returned a physical and emotional wreck, speaking little about the war and retreating into a haze of alcoholism. He and the other soldiers had been given atabrine, a wartime substitute for quinine, to ward off malaria. The medication left a ringing in his ears. It did not prevent reoccurring bouts of malaria. He would sit hunched and shaking next to my grandmother's white porcelain stove, convulsed by chills or fever. I remember him as a distant, bewildering man, struggling with demons I did not understand. His unit, I learned later, executed most of their prisoners. Like his great-grandfather David, he felt betrayed by his country, its generals, and its politicians. Maurice mailed his medals back to the Army. Seated at my grandmother's kitchen table one morning, he told me about the time his platoon was drinking from a stream. When they turned the corner, they saw twenty-five Japanese corpses in the water. It was the only time he spoke to me about his experiences in the South Pacific.

His erratic behavior was mystifying to me.

I asked my grandmother after he left what was wrong with him.

"The war," she said acidly.

XV.

Orphans

Lola Mozes's childhood came to an end in the fall of 1939 at a small bridge in Poland. She was nine, seated in a horse-drawn wagon, her back propped against her family's silver Sabbath candelabra, which was wrapped in a blanket, when she saw the aftermath of a German bomb attack. The sight of human bodies, along with eviscerated horses gasping in pain and struggling to rise despite their gaping wounds, reduced her to tears and panic. Her mother, Helena Rewitz, born Schwimer, who would hover over her daughter like a guardian angel later in a Jewish ghetto and the Auschwitz-Birkenau death camp, took the terrified child into her arms.

I sat with Lola Mozes at her dining room table in Brooklyn on a Friday. Short and petite, with curly black hair and white gold hoop earrings, she had a soft, infectious laugh, an impish sense of humor, and fine facial lines inherited from her father and mother. Her charm and warmth were girlish and slightly coquettish.

"I am the great pretender," she said, smiling. "It is always there, what I went through. I am tormented by it. It keeps repeating and repeating itself in my head."

Lola grew up living next to her family's small grocery in Katowice, a city in southwestern Poland. The language at home was German. She learned Polish in school. Her parents, especially when they wanted to talk privately, spoke Yiddish. Her parents and older brother celebrated the Sabbath and went to synagogue on religious holidays but lived as secular Jews. Her father, Emil, who sang arias as he bathed in the mornings, dressed in imported German suits and spats when he left the house. They lived in a working-class section of the city. Catholic children in the neighborhood taunted her as a "Christ killer" and once pushed her brother Oskar off a tram and beat him. But nothing prepared the family for what was to come. A dark future was only hinted at when the parents, their faces knotted in consternation, listened to Adolf Hitler on the radio.

The bloody scene at the bridge would foreshadow a crucible of mass murder and extreme deprivation lasting six years. For Lola, playing with her favorite doll, skating, swimming, and picking out candy from her father's grocery was replaced by a bitter struggle to survive. Ogres—including a drunken SS officer in the ghetto who used to hold her on his lap and complain about his boots being soiled by the blood of his victims, including the infants he dashed against walls—rose like monsters in medieval fairy tales. Concentric circles of death and life would radiate around her. Her parents' fierce love seemed, often, no match for the murderous intent of the armed and the powerful who held the family in their grip.

Lola's family was herded with other Jews in 1941 into the ghetto in Bochnia, along the river Raba in southern Poland. The ghetto was surrounded by a high wooden fence. It was divided in two parts—Ghetto A and Ghetto B. Ghetto A housed the 2,000 Jews who worked in German factories and workshops, where they made shoes, underwear, uniforms, gloves, socks, and other items for the German army. The Jews in Ghetto B had no jobs. Many were elderly and sick. They lived in extreme poverty and were malnourished. Many Jews pooled what little they had and formed communal kitchens. The Germans segregated the men, including the husbands and fathers, from women at night. Lola and her family lived with her aunt, who had been well off before the war, in a large wooden house that had been incorporated into the ghetto.

"At one point they told us to stay in our houses," she said. "I don't remember when. I peeked through the window and saw strong young men who used to work in the salt mines marching. Every tenth or fifth man was being shot. In the morning there was a strange odor. It was nauseating. We peeked through the curtains. There were wagons with dead bodies. They were stripped. There were puddles of blood in the gutters. We went back to work the following day. We worked twelve-hour shifts. For the morning shift we left when it was dark. I remember [when we went back to work again] it was raining. I was walking with my friend. I was carrying my bread. It fell on the ground. My friend said, 'It fell in the blood.' We thought this was very funny. We started laughing. I picked it up and brought it home after work and we ate it. It was too precious to throw away."

Lola had a friendship with a gentle boy who lived with his family in the B section of the ghetto. He cut up newspapers and made a little book he lent to her. It was about a seventh-century rabbi named Sabbatai Zevi who claimed to be the Jewish Messiah and walked from town to town promising to save the people. "He took me to where he lived," she said. "It looked like a hovel. There were rags on the floor. It was dirty. There were a lot of people, especially old people. The stench was terrible. He was the nicest boy. I said, 'How can people live like that?' He was so embarrassed. I will never forget how embarrassed he was. He had been in my aunt's house where each family had a room. My aunt's house was clean. We had a stove. There was some heat. I don't know what happened to him. Those in Ghetto B were the first to go in the transports [to the death camps]."

Her father constructed a small, underground bunker in a wooden shed that was filled with sawdust. When the deportations began in 1942 the family would hide in the bunker. There was barely enough room to huddle together. They would wait breathlessly as the Germans with their dogs prowled around the shed. Lola's father sneaked out at night to scavenge for food.

Jews could leave the ghetto only under guard. They were marched out of the ghetto in rows of five to work in German factories. Hans Frank, the governor-general of the territories in occupied Poland, ordered that any other Jews found outside ghetto walls be executed. Nearly 2,000 Jews from the ghetto were shot. Most of the others died from disease or in the death camps. Only 90 of the 15,000 people originally in the Bochnia ghetto survived the war.

Lola's father and brother worked cleaning German offices. She and her mother knitted socks for German soldiers in a large red brick building on Floris Street.

"They sent us socks from the Russian front," she said. "By the time the socks came to the factory they had been washed. The bottom parts had been cut off. Only the top part was left. We started knitting downwards to make a new sock. We sometimes found blood, toes, and parts of flesh in the socks. That is how we knew the Germans were struggling someplace where they were freezing."

One day the Jewish foreman at the knitting factory asked her to knit a pair of men's gloves. He gave her gray wool. A few weeks later a high-ranking group of Nazis visited the factory. Among them was Frank, whom the foreman introduced to Lola.

"He was wearing the gloves," she remembered. "He shook my hand. He smiled. He told me the gloves were keeping him very warm. He said they fit well. He thanked me. That evening my father came home from work. He was full of smiles. He told me everyone had been shaking his hand. They were congratulating him. Everyone said to him that because Frank shook your daughter's hand it would save the Jews. We thought if they were pleased with our work, they would let us live."

A year ago, she happened upon a picture of Frank. She learned, for the first time, that after the war he had been condemned and hanged by the Allies at Nuremberg. He was one of the very few Nazis at Nuremberg who, before being executed, expressed remorse for his crimes.

The photograph and news of Frank's execution were devastating. "I cried hysterically," she told me. "I don't know why. I could not connect him smiling at me like a father, shaking my hand and thanking me and then think of him hanging dead."

In the ghetto her parents arranged for her brother Oskar, who was two and a half years older, to study with a rabbi.

"My brother became, because of this rabbi, very orthodox," she said. "He was about fourteen. He would be charitable to everyone because the Bible said to be charitable. My mother would get some potatoes and peel them. She would say that when she came home from work, she would cook us potatoes. But sometimes the potatoes were gone when she got home. My brother would have taken them to a poor family, and we would have nothing to eat. One day he came home in wooden shoes. We asked, 'Where are your shoes?' He had given them to someone who was barefoot. He became like that. He was like a monk."

Once, hiding under the sawdust pile during one of the mass deportations, Lola crawled over to her brother. "We talked," she said. "It was the first time we really talked. He had a piece of bread. He said, 'I am not hungry.'"

Her voice broke. She began to weep.

"That is hard," she said haltingly. "And he did give me that piece of bread. It was like a rind. We were not like sheep. We lived. When we finally left the bunker, I saw him dressing. His belly was distended from hunger."

The factories and workshops were closed in 1943. Large sections of the ghetto were emptied. Most of the ghetto residents had been executed or taken to death camps. When Lola's father sneaked out of the bunker at night he would wander through empty streets and forage in abandoned apartments. It resembled a ghost town. The fence around the ghetto was being rebuilt and pushed inward to open the emptied sections of the ghetto to the non-Jews in the city.

Lola's father decided to move the family, along with her aunt's family of four and two cousins, to a basement in an abandoned part of the ghetto. He said that when it got dark, he would take five of them at a time to the basement. He took Lola, her mother, Lola's aunt, and a young cousin to the basement and went back to get his son and nieces and nephews.

"He never returned," Lola said. "He was captured by a Jewish policeman. It was Succoth. My mother and aunt lit candles in the basement. We found a deeper basement. There was an Orthodox man hidden in the attic of that house. He visited us. He told us stories about the Messiah. He told us when we died, we would go to heaven. I felt better, even with that gripping fear. My cousin and I went out at night to a vegetable field to dig up something to eat. There was a well, but it made noise when you cranked it up. That was dangerous. We could hear dogs barking.

"One morning we heard a sound like someone scraping a stick along a fence," she said. "My mother stiffened. She knew. They were shooting people. We could see the man in the attic make a sign with his arms like shooting. Then we heard singing. It was Shema Yisrael."

She began to sing Shema Yisrael, the central prayer in the Jewish prayer book, softly in Hebrew.

> *Hear, O Israel: The Lord our God is one Lord.*
> *And thou shalt love the Lord thy God with all thine heart, and*
>   *with all thy soul, and with all thy might.*
> *And these words which I command thee this day shall be in*
>   *thine heart.*

"There were two hundred people singing Shema Yisrael, including my father and brother, going to death," she said. "I did not at the time connect the shooting with my father and brother and cousins. The shots became steady and constant. My mother held me tight."

Lola read from a letter she wrote in 1981 to her four children:

> Here is the essence of my story. To help my children grow, flourish and multiply without guilt or remorse, without a feeling that they are descended of people who went to slaughter like sheep. No song like Eli Eli

or Ave Maria will surpass the chant of my father, my brother, my cousins, and hundreds of others as they were led to be shot. It was the most powerful, courageous, and victorious hymn. Their voices did not bleat like sheep. Their voices told of victory overcoming evil by dying like men without somebody's blood on their hands. Their voices sang in unison a praise to the Lord. There was a might in them as if they were already one with their master. And it said Shema Yisrael, Hear Oh Israel, I will take you from your suffering and you will flourish. This was the message I received. That song was sung for me by my father. I flourished as I wish and hope my children will. My children, my dear sweet children. Your daily problems, which you try to solve with so much determination, are insignificant in the view of the awesome past of your ancestors. So you are told, but this is not true. Life is made out of difficulties and joys, of sorrows and utter happiness, but as long as your souls are not soiled with meanness which hurts others, be proud of your life. Your life is the extension of the ones which are gone. And now they are immortal. Don't pity them. They went peacefully because they had hope for the future, your present. My father's mighty chant was meant as well for you and yours. With all my love, your mom.

German soldiers discovered Lola, her mother, her aunt, and her cousin in the basement. They were detained and, because hiding was a capital offense, waited to be shot. Her mother, holding her, told Lola they were going to the Garden of Eden to meet those in the family who had died. But they were spared and assigned to the last detail of one hundred Jews used to clean up the remnants of the ghetto. The mother, working in a laundry, found her son Oskar's shirt, apparently cut from his lifeless body. Josef Müller, the commander of the ghetto, had by then a Jewish mistress, a practice common among ghetto commanders and camp guards. The remaining Jews in the ghetto nicknamed her Mata Hari.

"She was quite beautiful, very tall," Lola said. "She was dressed elegantly and wore makeup. She had a husband and a daughter my age. She ordered me around. I had to clean her room."

Lola and her mother were then sent to the labor camp in Plaszów, a southern suburb of Kraków. Plaszów was commanded by Amon Göth, a brutal SS officer who routinely shot prisoners for sport and was portrayed in the 1993 film *Schindler's List*. Göth was hanged after the war.

Lola and her mother were put to work with other prisoners digging up a Jewish cemetery. The headstones were used for paving roads and constructing latrines. After spending two months in Plaszów they were sent to work in a munitions factory hidden in a forest near Pionki. It was there Lola was forced to watch the hanging of four or five Jews who had tried to escape. She took her mother's place in the front of the formation of prisoners to spare her the sight of the hangings.

"They were calm and collected," Lola said of the condemned. "They had their hands tied behind their backs. They said something before they died, but I don't remember what. We were ordered to look at the hanging. We could not turn away our heads. As I watched, I saw what a horrific death it is—you can actually see life being squeezed out of the body. The face purple, red, almost swelling, as the hanging body twitches in last rebellion. The wife of one of the men, belly swollen with child, stood by the gallows the whole week as the Germans kept the spectacle on display."

Lola was eventually transported to Auschwitz-Birkenau. The journey by train took three days. When she stumbled off the train with her mother, aunt, and cousin, she ran toward a ditch to get a drink of water. She visited Auschwitz-Birkenau years later and searched out the ditch. She said the death camp stripped of the emaciated bodies, stench, fear, shootings, barking dogs, beatings, smoke from the crematoriums, shouts of the guards, overcrowded barracks, and foul, overflowing latrines failed to convey its reality. "They should plow it under and plant a field," she said.

"I did not recognize my mother when we got off the train," she remembered of her arrival at the camp. "She scared me. It was like seeing a ghost. She was drawn. She had big, round eyes."

They were quarantined in Camp C after being shaved, sprayed with DDT, and tattooed. She remembers seeing a group of dwarfs in the camp. "They were so beautiful," she said. "I wanted to play with them. They were like dolls. On the second or third night they all disappeared."

She and her mother spent about eight months working in Birkenau. At one point they were stripped and forced into a gas chamber with a large group of women before the execution was abruptly canceled. Lola had begged her mother before entering the gas chamber for their last piece of bread. "I said, 'I don't want to die hungry,'" she remembered. "My mother, said, 'When we come out you will tell me you are hungry.' I said, 'I don't care.' And she gave me the bread. When we got out of the gas chamber my mother said, 'I told you so.'" The women were later put to work twisting strips of oilcloth into braids to be used, she believed, to make plane doors airtight.

"Two guards would pull on the ends of the braid, and if it broke the workers would be beaten, often to death," she said.

In January 1945, with Soviet forces advancing on occupied Poland, the Nazi guards began to plan the destruction of the crematoria. They told the prisoners the Birkenau camp would be dynamited, and ordered some 60,000 prisoners from Birkenau and the satellite camps to begin a thirty-five-mile march through the snow to a freight yard. Fifteen thousand prisoners died on the march. Lola's aunt and cousin, who survived the war, hid under a pile of corpses. Lola and her mother, shortly before joining the march, found turnips in a barracks, and gorged themselves. The turnips gave her mother diarrhea.

Lola recounted:

My mother ripped a piece of her dress and asked me very shyly the next morning if I could wash her off, and that is when I felt what love is. She told me they would dynamite the camp and we should leave, that I could withstand the march. We walked through the night. We passed our town, Katowice. We saw the lights. The next day my mother wasn't feeling good. She was dizzy. She asked me for a little sugar. We were not allowed to bend down for snow. If you bent down, they would shoot you. There were bodies on the sides of the road. But my mother asked me for some snow. I bent down quickly to get her some snow. The women around us helped my mother for a little while. They walked with her. Then my mother couldn't walk. There was a tree. She lay down. She told me, "Run quickly and maybe you will save yourself." Then a German materialized. I fought with him. I told him, "You have a mother. You know what it means to have a mother. Let her rest a minute and she will be able to get up." He smiled. I will always remember that strange smile. Something amused him. By that time his pistol was drawn. The soldiers began to hit me and push me away. He shot her. I was on the road again. At one point my little sack fell down. I picked it up. I thought to myself, you picked up the sack, but you did not pick up your mother. Years later, as I replayed the scene of my mother's death, her laying, reclining under that tree with her arms a bit outstretched, I thought of her as being crucified.

Lola made it to the freight yard and was loaded onto one of the open cars. She was transported to Ravensbrück, a women's concentration camp in northern Germany. She was then put on a train to the Malhof camp. As Allied soldiers neared Malhof, the Germans closed the camp. Lola was soon marching again. Then the guards began to disappear. She remembers the bloated and blackened bodies of soldiers in the fields. One morning she and the other prisoners saw the camp commander in civilian clothes riding away on a bicycle. The war was over.

There is, somewhere in the vastness of the universe, amid galaxies and stars that light emanating from our planet takes decades to reach, the airy image of a girl playing with a doll in the Polish town of Katowice, the image of a girl terrified and clutched by her mother near a bombed bridge, the image of a girl hiding with her brother under a pile of sawdust and accepting a small piece of bread, the image of a girl shaking the hand of the Nazi governor of Poland, and the image of a girl in her mother's arms in a basement listening to men and women about to die singing Shema Yisrael. There is, too, the image of a girl telling a German soldier with a drawn pistol, "You have a mother."

"I believe in God and heaven," Lola said last week. "I speak to my husband, who I lost three years ago, and my parents. My belief saves me from talking to walls and air."

I did not write this story to say that Germans are bad, and Jews are good. The line between good and evil runs through all hearts. It is, sadly, as easy to become an executioner as a victim. This is the most sobering lesson of war. And it is something the greatest writers on the Holocaust, such as Primo Levi, understood. There were, after all, *Jüdische Ghetto-Polizei*, Jewish *Kapos*, Judenräte, Sonderkommandos, and Blockälteste whose contributions to the organization of the ghettos and the death camps kept the crematoria functioning. The prisoners who lowered themselves to the moral squalor of the SS were soon lost. I did not write this piece to say that virtue or goodness triumphed after the Holocaust. The Nazi extermination of twelve million people, including six million Jews, was a colossal, tragic, and absurd waste of human life. I wrote this piece to say that the fierce and protective love of a mother and a father is stronger than hate. It can overcome evil. After the war Lola met a young German man in Spain. "He could have been a soldier," she said. He asked Lola about her wartime experience. She told him. She kissed him on the cheek in saying goodbye.

Where time and light bend and twist in space, perhaps defying the known laws of physics, a mother, and a father, fighting to protect their daughter and son from death, still exist in faint particles of light, making visible an iron bond of fidelity. They gave up life to save it. Scarred emotionally and physically—she rolled up her sleeve as we talked to show me her tattooed concentration camp number, A-14989—Lola would nevertheless marry a survivor to raise, love, and nurture four children of her own. Emil Rewitz and Helena Rewitz, at least in this small house in Brooklyn, won the war.

XVI.

Permanent War

Permanent war, which has defined the United States since World War II, extinguishes liberal, democratic movements. It cheapens culture into nationalist cant. It degrades and corrupts education and the media and wrecks the economy. The liberal, democratic forces, tasked with maintaining an open society, become impotent.

It was a decline into permanent war, not Islam, that killed the liberal, democratic movements in the Arab world, ones that held great promise in the early part of the twentieth century in countries such as Egypt, Syria, Lebanon, and Iran. It is a state of permanent war that is finishing off the liberal traditions in Israel and the United States.

"War," Randolph Bourne commented acidly, "is the health of the state."[77]

"The moment war is declared, however, the mass of the people, through some spiritual alchemy, become convinced that they have willed and executed the deed themselves," Bourne wrote. "They then with the exception of a few malcontents, proceed to allow themselves to be regimented, coerced, deranged in all the environments of their lives, and turned into a solid manufactory of destruction toward whatever other people may have, in the appointed scheme of things, come within the range of the Government's disapprobation. The citizen throws off his contempt and indifference to Government, identifies himself with its purposes, revives all his military memories and symbols, and the State once more walks, an august presence, through the imaginations of men. Patriotism becomes the dominant feeling, and produces immediately that intense and hopeless confusion between the relations which the individual bears and should bear towards the society of which he is a part."[78]

In *Pentagon Capitalism: The Political Economy of War* Seymour Melman described the defense industry as viral. Defense and military industries in permanent war, he wrote, distort economies. They upend social and economic priorities. They redirect government expenditures toward their huge military projects and starve domestic investment in the name of national security. We produce sophisticated fighter jets, while Boeing is unable to finish its new commercial plane on schedule. Our automotive industry goes bankrupt. We sink money into research and development of weapons systems and neglect renewable energy technologies to fight global warming. Universities are flooded with defense-related cash and grants, and struggle to find money for environmental studies. This is the disease of permanent war.

Massive military spending in this country, climbing to nearly $1 trillion a year and consuming half of all discretionary spending, has a profound social cost. Bridges and levees collapse. Schools decay. Domestic manufacturing declines. Trillions in debts threaten the viability of the currency and the economy. The poor, the mentally ill, the sick and the unemployed are abandoned. Human suffering, including our own, is the price for victory.

Citizens in a state of permanent war are bombarded with the insidious militarized language of power, fear, and strength that masks an increasingly brittle reality. The corporations behind the doctrine of permanent war—who have corrupted Leon Trotsky's doctrine of permanent revolution—must keep us afraid. Fear stops us from objecting to government spending on a bloated military. Fear means we will not ask unpleasant questions of those in power. Fear means that we will be willing to give up our rights and liberties for security. Fear keeps us penned in like domesticated animals.

Melman, who coined the term *permanent war economy* to characterize the American economy, wrote that since the end of the Second World War, the federal government has spent more than half its tax dollars on past, current, and future military operations. It is the largest single sustaining activity of the government. The military-industrial establishment is a very lucrative business. It is gilded corporate welfare. Defense systems are sold before they are produced. Military industries are permitted to charge the federal government for huge cost overruns. Massive profits are always guaranteed.

Foreign aid is given to countries such as Egypt, which receives some $3 billion in assistance and is required to buy American weapons with $1.3 billion of the money. The taxpayers fund the research, development, and building of weapons systems and then buy them on behalf of foreign governments. It is a bizarre circular system. It defies the concept of a free-market economy. These weapons systems are soon in need of being updated or replaced. They are hauled, years later, into junkyards, where they are left to rust. It is, in economic terms, a dead end. It sustains nothing but the permanent war economy.

Those who profit from permanent war are not restricted

by the economic rules of producing goods, selling them for a profit, then using the profit for further investment and production. They operate, rather, outside of competitive markets. They erase the line between the state and the corporation. They leech away the ability of the nation to manufacture useful products and produce sustainable jobs. Melman used the example of the New York City Transit Authority and its allocation in 2003 of $3 billion to $4 billion for new subway cars. New York City asked for bids, and no American companies responded. Melman argued that the industrial base in America was no longer centered on items that maintain, improve, or are used to build the nation's infrastructure. New York City eventually contracted with companies in Japan and Canada to build its subway cars. Melman estimated that such a contract could have generated, directly and indirectly, about 32,000 jobs in the United States. In another instance, of one hundred products offered in the 2003 L.L.Bean catalogue, Melman found that ninety two were imported and only eight were made in the United States.

The late senator J. William Fulbright described the reach of the military-industrial establishment in his 1970 book *The Pentagon Propaganda Machine*. Fulbright explained how the Pentagon influenced and shaped public opinion through multimillion-dollar public relations campaigns, Defense Department films, close ties with Hollywood producers, and use of the commercial media. Most of the military analysts on television are former military officials, many employed as consultants to defense industries, a fact they rarely disclose to the public. As reported in the *New York Times*, Barry R. McCaffrey, a retired four-star Army general and military analyst for NBC News, was at the same time an employee of Defense Solutions

Inc., a consulting firm. He profited, the article noted, from the sale of the weapons systems and expansion of the wars in Iraq and Afghanistan he championed over the airwaves.

Our permanent war economy has bipartisan support. The two ruling parties support its destructive fury because it funds them. To challenge the military-industrial complex is political suicide.

A state of permanent war, which has defined the United States since World War II, means the inevitable death of liberalism. Dick Cheney may be palpably evil while Joe Biden is merely weak, but to those who seek to keep us in a state of permanent war, it does not matter. They get what they want. Fyodor Dostoevsky wrote *Notes from Underground* to illustrate what happens to cultures when a liberal class, like ours, becomes a block of sterile, defeated dreamers. The main character in *Notes from Underground* carries the bankrupt ideas of liberalism to their logical extreme. He becomes the enlightenment ideal. He eschews passion and moral purpose. He is rational. He prizes realism over sanity, even in the face of self-destruction. These acts of accommodation doom the Underground Man, as it doomed imperial Russia and as it will doom us.

"I never even managed to become anything: neither wicked nor good, neither a scoundrel nor an honest man, neither a hero nor an insect," the Underground Man wrote. "And now I am living out my life in my corner, taunting myself with the spiteful and utterly futile consolation that it is even impossible for an intelligent man seriously to become anything, and only fools become something."[79]

The decline of the American empire began long before the current economic meltdown or the wars in Afghanistan and Iraq. It began before the first Gulf War of Ronald Reagan. It began when we shifted, in the words of the historian Charles Maier, from an "empire of production" to an "empire of consumption."[80] By the end of the Vietnam War, when the costs of the war ate away at Lyndon Johnson's Great Society and domestic oil production began its steady, inexorable decline, we saw our country transformed from one that primarily produced to one that primarily consumed. We started borrowing to maintain a lifestyle we could no longer afford. We began to use force, especially in the Middle East, to feed our insatiable demand for cheap oil. The years after World War II, when the United States accounted for one-third of world exports and half of the world's manufacturing, gave way to huge trade imbalances, outsourced jobs, rusting hulks of abandoned factories, stagnant wages, and personal and public debts that most of us cannot repay.

The bill is now due. America's most dangerous enemies are not Islamic radicals, but those who promote the perverted ideology of national security that, as Andrew Bacevich wrote, is "our surrogate religion."[81] If we continue to believe that we can expand our wars and go deeper into debt to maintain an unsustainable level of consumption, we will dynamite the foundations of our society.

"The Big Lies are not the pledge of tax cuts, universal health care, family values restored, or a world rendered peaceful through forceful demonstrations of American leadership," Bacevich wrote in *The Limits of Power: The End of American Exceptionalism.* "The Big Lies are the truths that remain unspoken: that freedom has an underside; that nations, like households, must ultimately live within their means; that history's purpose, the subject of so many confident pronouncements, remains inscrutable. Above all, there is this: Power is finite. Politicians pass over matters such as these in silence. Consequently, the absence of self-awareness that forms such an enduring element of the American character persists."

The expansion of NATO into Central and Eastern Europe has earned Lockheed Martin Corp., Raytheon Technologies Corp., General Dynamics Corp., Boeing Co., Northrop Grumman Corp., Analytic Services Inc., Huntington Ingalls Industries Inc., Humana Inc., BAE Systems, and L3Harris Technologies Inc. billions in profits. The stoking of conflict in Ukraine will earn them billions more. The invasion of Ukraine saw the stocks of General Dynamics, Lockheed Martin, Northrup Grumman, and Raytheon hit a fifty-two-week high.

The European Union has allocated hundreds of millions of euros to purchase weapons for Ukraine. Germany will almost triple its defense budget. The Biden administration has asked Congress to provide $6.4 billion in funding to assist Ukraine, supplementing the $650 million in military aid to Ukraine over the past year. The permanent war economy operates outside the laws of supply and demand. It is the root of the two-decade-long quagmire in the Middle East. It is the root of the conflict with Moscow. The merchants of death are satanic. The more corpses they produce, the more their bank accounts swell. They will cash in on this conflict, one that now flirts with the nuclear holocaust that will terminate life on earth as we know it.

The dangerous and sadly predictable provocation of Russia—whose nuclear arsenal places the sword of Damocles above our heads—by expanding NATO was understood by all of us who reported in Central and Eastern Europe in 1989 during the revolutions and the breakup of the Soviet Union.

This provocation, which includes establishing a NATO missile base one hundred miles from Russia's border, was foolish and highly irresponsible. It never made geopolitical sense. This does not, however, excuse the invasion of Ukraine. Yes, the Russians were baited. But they reacted by pulling the trigger. This is a crime. Their crime. Let us pray for a ceasefire. Let us work for a return to diplomacy and sanity, a moratorium on arms shipments to Ukraine. Let us hope for an end to war before we stumble into a nuclear holocaust that devours us all.

The vain effort to purify the world through force is always self-defeating. Those who insist that the world can be molded into their vision are the most susceptible to violence as antidote. The more uncertainty, fear, and reality impinge on this utopian vision, the more strident, absolutist, and aggressive are those who call for the eradication of "the enemy." Immanuel Kant called absolute moral imperatives that are used to carry out immoral acts "a radical evil." He wrote that this kind of evil was always a form of unadulterated self-love. It was the worst type of self-deception. It provided a moral façade for terror and murder.

In endless war it does not matter whom we fight. Endless war is not about winning battles or promoting a cause. It is an end. In George Orwell's novel *Nineteen Eighty-Four*, Oceania is at war with Eurasia and allied with Eastasia. The alliance is then suddenly reversed. Eurasia becomes an ally of Oceania, and Eastasia is the enemy. The point is not who is being fought. The point is maintaining a state of fear and the mass mobilization of the public. War and national security are used to justify the surrender of citizenship, the crushing of dissent, and expanding the powers of the state. The point is war itself. And if the American state, once a sworn enemy of Hezbollah, gives air cover to Hezbollah fighters in Syria, the goals of endless war remain gloriously untouched.

But endless war is not sustainable. States that wage endless war inevitably collapse. They drain their treasuries, are hated by the wretched of the earth, and militarize and strangle their political, social, and cultural life while impoverishing and repressing their populations. They are seduced by what Sigmund Freud called the "death instinct." This is where we are headed. The only question is when it will unravel.

Edward Gibbon observed about the Roman Empire's own lust for endless war, "[T]he decline of Rome was the natural and inevitable effect of immoderate greatness. Prosperity ripened the principle of decay; the cause of the destruction multiplied with the extent of conquest; and, as soon as time or accident had removed the artificial supports, the stupendous fabric yielded to the pressure of its own weight. The story of the ruin is simple and obvious: and instead of inquiring *why* the Roman Empire was destroyed we should rather be surprised that it had subsisted for so long."[82]

The ruling corporate elites no longer seek to build. They seek to destroy. They are agents of death. They crave the unimpeded power to cannibalize the country and pollute and degrade the ecosystem to feed an insatiable lust for wealth, power, and hedonism. Wars and military "virtues" are celebrated. Intelligence, empathy, and the common good are banished. Culture is degraded to patriotic kitsch. Education is designed only to instill technical proficiency to serve the poisonous engine of corporate capitalism. Historical amnesia shuts us off from the past, the present, and the future. Those branded as unproductive or redundant are discarded and left to struggle in poverty or locked away in cages. State repression is indiscriminate and brutal.

The graveyard of world empires—Sumerian, Egyptian, Greek, Roman, Mayan, Khmer, Ottoman, and Austro-Hungarian—followed the same trajectory of moral and physical collapse.

Sigmund Freud wrote that societies, along with individuals, are driven by two primary instincts. One is the instinct for life, Eros, the quest to love, nurture, protect, and preserve. The second is the death instinct. The death instinct, called Thanatos by post-Freudians, is driven by fear, hatred, and violence. It seeks the dissolution of all living things, including our own beings. One of these two forces, Freud wrote, is always ascendant. Societies in decline enthusiastically embrace the death instinct, as Freud observed in *Civilization and Its Discontents*, written on the eve of the rise of European fascism and World War II.

"It is in sadism, where the death instinct twists the erotic aim in its own sense and yet at the same time fully satisfies the erotic urge, that we succeed in obtaining the clearest insight into its nature and its relation to *Eros*," Freud wrote. "But even where it emerges without any sexual purpose, in the blindest fury of destructiveness, we cannot fail to recognize that the satisfaction of the instinct is accompanied by an extraordinarily high degree of narcissistic enjoyment, owing to its presenting the ego with a fulfillment of the latter's old wishes for omnipotence."[83]

The lust for death, as Freud understood, is not, at first, morbid. It is exciting and seductive. I saw this in the wars I covered. A god-like power and adrenaline-driven fury, even euphoria, sweep over armed units and ethnic or religious groups given the license to destroy anything and anyone around them. Ernst Jünger captured this "monstrous desire for annihilation" in his World War I memoir, *Storm of Steel*. A population alienated and beset by despair and hopelessness finds empowerment and pleasure in an orgy of annihilation that morphs into self-annihilation. It has no interest in nurturing a world that has betrayed it and thwarted its dreams.

It seeks to eradicate this world and replace it with a mythical landscape. It turns against institutions, as well as ethnic and religious groups, that are scapegoated for its misery. It plunders diminishing natural resources with abandon. It is seduced by the fantastic promises of demagogues and the magical solutions characteristic of the Christian right or what anthropologists call "crisis cults."

Human motives often are irrational and, as Freud pointed out, contain powerful yearnings for death and self-immolation. Science and technology have empowered and amplified the ancient lusts for war, violence, and death. Knowledge did not free humankind from barbarism. The civilized veneer only masked the dark, inchoate longings that plague all human societies, including our own. Freud feared the destructive power of these urges. He warned in *Civilization and Its Discontents* that if we could not regulate or contain these urges, human beings would, as the Stoics predicted, consume themselves in a vast conflagration. The future of humanity depends on naming and controlling these urges. To pretend they do not exist is to fall into self-delusion.

The breakdown of social and political control during periods of political and economic turmoil allows these urges to reign supreme. Our first inclination, Freud noted correctly, is not to love one another as brothers or sisters but to "satisfy [our] aggressiveness on [our fellow human being], to exploit his capacity for work without compensation, to use him sexually without his consent, to seize his possessions, to humiliate him, to cause him pain, to torture and to kill him."[84] The war in Bosnia, with rampaging Serbian militias, rape camps, torture centers, concentration camps, razed villages, and mass executions, was one of numerous examples of Freud's wisdom. At best, Freud knew, we can learn to live with, regulate, and control our inner tensions and conflicts. The structure of civilized societies would always be fraught with this inner tension, he wrote, because "man's natural aggressive instinct, the hostility of each against all and of all against each, opposes this program of civilization." The burden of civilization is worth it. The alternative, as Freud knew, is self-destruction.

Mary Shelley warned us about becoming Prometheus as we seek to defy fate and the gods to master life and death. Her Victor Frankenstein, when his eight-foot-tall creation made partly of body pieces from graves came to ghastly life, had the same reaction as J. Robert Oppenheimer when the American scientist discovered that his bomb had incinerated Japanese schoolchildren. The scientist Victor Frankenstein watched the "dull yellow eye" of his creature open and "breathless horror and disgust filled his heart." Oppenheimer said after the first atomic bomb was detonated in the New Mexican desert: "I remembered the line from the Hindu scripture, the Bhagavad-Gita. Vishnu is trying to persuade the prince that he should do his duty and to impress him takes on his multi-armed form and says, 'Now I am become Death, the destroyer of worlds.' I suppose we all thought that, in one way or another."[85] The critic Harold Bloom, in words that could be applied to Oppenheimer, called Victor Frankenstein "a moral idiot."

All attempts to control the universe, to play God, to become the arbiters of life and death, have been carried out by moral idiots. They will relentlessly push forward, exploiting and pillaging, perfecting their terrible tools of technology and science, until their creation destroys them and us. They make the nuclear bombs. They extract oil from the tar sands.

They turn the Appalachians into a wasteland to extract coal. They serve the evils of globalism and finance. They run the fossil fuel industry. They flood the atmosphere with carbon emissions, doom the seas, melt the polar ice caps, unleash the droughts and floods, the heat waves, the freak storms and hurricanes.

Coda

I carry within me death. The smell of decayed and bloated corpses. The cries of the wounded. The shrieks of children. The sound of gunfire. The deafening blasts. The fear. The stench of cordite. The humiliation that comes when you surrender to terror and beg for life. The loss of comrades and friends. And then the aftermath. The long alienation. The numbness. The nightmares. The lack of sleep. The inability to connect to all living things, even to those we love the most. The regret. The absurdity. The waste. The futility.

It is only the broken and the maimed that know war. We ask for forgiveness. We seek redemption. We carry on our backs this awful cross of death, for the essence of war is death, and the weight of it digs into our shoulders and eats away at our souls. We drag it through life, up hills and down hills, along the roads, into the most intimate recesses of our lives. It never leaves us. Those who know us best know that there is something unspeakable and evil many of us harbor within us. This evil is intimate. It is personal. We do not speak its name. It is the evil of things done and things left undone. It is the evil of war.

War is captured in the long, vacant stares, in the silences, in the trembling fingers, in the memories most of us keep buried deep within us, in the tears.

It is impossible to portray war. Narratives, even anti-war narratives, make the irrational rational. They make the incomprehensible comprehensible. They make the illogical logical. They make the despicable beautiful. All words and images, all discussions, all films, all evocations of war, good or bad, are an obscenity. There is nothing to say. There are only the scars and wounds. These we carry within us. These we cannot articulate. The horror. The horror.

I wander through life with the deadness of war within me. There is no escape. There is no peace. All of us who have been to war know an awful truth. Ghosts. Strangers in a strange land.

Who are our brothers and sisters? Who is our family? Whom have we become?

We have become those whom we once despised and killed. We have become the enemy. Our mother is the mother grieving over her murdered child, and we murdered this child, in a mud-walled village of Afghanistan, a sand-filled cemetery in Fallujah or Mariupol. Our father is the father lying on a pallet in a hut, paralyzed by the blast from an iron fragmentation bomb. Our sister lives in poverty in a refugee camp outside Kabul, widowed, desperately poor, raising her children alone. Our brother, yes, our brother, is in the Taliban and the Iraqi insurgency and al-Qaida and the Russian soldiers. And he has an automatic rifle. And he kills. And he is becoming us. War is always the same plague. It imparts the same deadly virus. It teaches us to deny another's humanity, worth, being, and to kill and be killed.

There are days I wish I was whole. I wish I could put down this cross. I envy those who, in their innocence, believe in the innate goodness of America and the righteousness of war, and celebrate what we know is despicable. Sometimes it makes me wish for death, for the peace of it. But I know the awful truth, as James Baldwin wrote, that "people who shut their eyes to reality simply invite their own destruction, and anyone who insists on remaining in a state of innocence long after that innocence is dead turns himself into a monster."[86] And I would rather be maimed and broken and in pain than a monster.

I will never be healed. I cannot promise that it will be better. I cannot impart to you the cheerful and childish optimism that is the curse of America. I can only tell you to stand up, to pick up your cross, to keep moving. I can only tell you that you must always defy the forces that eat away at you, at the nation—this plague of war.

Sometimes I feel like a motherless child
A long ways from home
A long ways from home

It is death I defy, not my own death, but the vast enterprise of death. The dark, primeval lusts for power and personal wealth, the hypermasculine language of war and patriotism, used to justify the slaughter of the weak and the innocent and to mock justice. I do not use these words.

We cannot flee from evil. Some of us who have been to war have tried, through drink and drugs and self-destructiveness. Evil is always with us. It is because we know evil, our own evil, that we do not let go, do not surrender. It is because we know evil that we resist. It is because we know violence that we are nonviolent. And we know that it is not about us. War taught us that. It is about the other, lying by the side of the road. It is about reaching down in defiance of creeds and oaths, in defiance of religion and nationality, and lifting our enemy up. All acts of healing and love—and the defiance of war is an affirmation of love—allow us to shout out to the vast powers of the universe that, however broken we are, we are not helpless, however much we despair we are not without hope, however weak we may feel, we will always, always, always resist.

ACKNOWLEDGMENTS

Those who gave me interviews for this book did so at great emotional cost. They spoke about the most traumatic and painful events in their lives. What power there is in this book comes from them. I owe all of them, many of whom have become friends, a tremendous debt. I admire them for their fortitude and courage. They speak a hard truth. We must all listen.

Lola Mozes spent many hours with me reliving the suffering she endured in her childhood—which saw her father, mother, and brother killed in the Holocaust—and the horror of the Auschwitz-Birkenau death camp. Tomas and Claudia Young invited me into their home in the last days of Tomas's life as he made one final and noble stand against the politicians who lied to him and to other young men and women they sent to Iraq. I want to thank the veterans Spenser Rapone, Rory Fanning, Michael Hanes, Robert Weilbacher, Joshua Morgan Folmar, Brian Turner, George Kovach, Geoffrey Millard, Ben Flanders, Josh Middleton, Camilo Mejía, Phillip Chrystal, Jessica Goodell, as well as Boyah J. Farah and Carlos Arredondo. They bear the terrible and lifelong wounds of war.

Eunice, who raises everything I write to a higher level, was, as always, my muse, although sometimes a blunt and demanding one. Thomas Caswell, one of the finest copy editors in the business, and the two great journalists Robert Scheer and Narda

Zacchino devoted many hours to the copy. I also want to thank Chris Scheer and Christopher Renshaw for their assistance, as well as the very talented copy editor Elizabeth Bell. Dan Simon, the publisher of Seven Stories Press, and Greg Ruggiero from City Lights were instrumental in putting this project together. I am glad they pushed me to do it. Finally, I want to thank my family for putting up with my manic writing schedule, and our two lazy greyhounds, who usually lie a couple of feet away from me as I hammer away at the keyboard.

BIBLIOGRAPHY

Adorno, Theodor. *Critical Models: Interventions and Catchwords*. New York: Columbia University Press, 2005.

Auden, W. H. *Selected Poems*. London: Faber and Faber, 1979.

Bacevich, Andrew J. *The Limits of Power: The End of American Exceptionalism*. New York: Metropolitan Books, 2008.

Baldwin, James. "Stranger in the Village." In *The Collected Essays of James Baldwin*. New York: The Library of America, 1998.

Bartov, Omer. *Mirrors of Destruction: War, Genocide, and Modern Identity*. New York: Oxford University Press, 2000.

————. *Murder in Our Midst: The Holocaust, Industrial Killing, and Repression*. New York: Oxford University Press, 1996.

Benda, Julien, *The Treason of the Intellectuals*. New Brunswick: Transaction Publishers, 2009.

Bird, Kai, and Martin J. Sherwin. *American Prometheus: The Triumph and Tragedy of J. Robert Oppenheimer*. New York: Vintage Books, 2005.

Bonner, Raymond. "The Diplomat and the Killer." *The Atlantic*, February 11, 2016. https://www.theatlantic.com/international/archive/2016/02/el-salvador-churchwomen-murders/460320/.

Bourne, Randolph. *War and the Intellectuals*. Indianapolis: Hackett Publishing Company, Inc., 1999

Curtis, O. E. *History of the 24th Michigan of Iron Brigade*. Detroit: Winn & Hammond, 1891.

Dostoevsky, Fyodor. *Notes from Underground*. New York: Alfred A. Knopf, 1993.

Findley, Timothy. *Inside Memory: Pages from a Writer's Workbook*. Toronto: HarperCollins Publishers Ltd., 1990.

Foote, Shelby. *Stars in Their Courses: The Gettysburg Campaign, June–July 1863*. New York: Random House, 1994.

Friedman, Thomas. Interview by Charlie Rose. *Charlie Rose* (May 30, 2003). https://charlierose.com/episodes/26893.

Freud, Sigmund. *Civilization and Its Discontents.* New York: W. W. Norton, 1989.

Friedrich, Ernst. *War against War.* Seattle, WA: The Real Comet Press, 1987.

Fulbright, J. William, *The Pentagon Propaganda Machine.* New York: Vintage Books, 1971.

Fussell, Paul. *The Great War and Modern Memory.* New York: Sterling Publishing Company, Inc., 2009.

———. *Wartime: Understanding and Behavior in the Second World War.* New York: Oxford University Press, 1989.

García Márquez, Gabriel. *Chronicle of a Death Foretold.* New York: Alfred A. Knopf, 1983.

Gibbon, Edward. *The Decline and Fall of The Roman Empire*, vol. II. New York: Modern Library, 2005.

Gibbs, Philip. *Now It Can Be Told.* New York: Harper & Brothers, 1920.

Goodell, Jess, with John Hearn. *Shade it Black: Death and After in Iraq.* Havertown, PA: Casemate Publishers, 2011.

Gray, J. Glenn. *The Warriors: Reflections on Men in Battle.* Lincoln: University of Nebraska Press, 1998.

Grinker, Lori. *Afterwar: Veterans from a World in Conflict.* de.mo design limited, 2005.

Grossman, David. *On Killing: The Psychological Cost of Learning to Kill in War and Society.* Boston: Little, Brown, 1996.

Grossman, Vasily. *Everything Flows.* New York: New York Review Book, 2009.

Guelzo, Allen C. *Gettysburg: The Last Invasion.* New York: Vintage Books, 2013.

Hedges, Chris, and Laila Al-Arian. *Collateral Damage: America's War against Iraqi Civilians.* New York: Nation Books, 2008.

Hedges, Chris. *War is a Force That Gives Us Meaning.* New York: Public Affairs, 2014.

———. *What Every Person Should Know about War.* New York: Free Press, 2003.

Herman, Edward S., and Noam Chomsky. *Manufacturing Consent: The Political Economy of the Mass Media.* New York: Pantheon Books, 1988.

Hochschild, Adam. *To End All Wars: A Story of Loyalty and Rebellion, 1914–1918.* New York: Mariner Books, 2011.

Hynes, Samuel. *The Soldier's Tale.* New York: Penguin, 1997.

Jones, Franklin D. *Textbook of Military Medicine.* Falls Church, VA: Office of the Army Surgeon General, U.S. Army, 1995.

Jünger, Ernst. *Storm of Steel: From the Diary of a German Storm-troop Officer on the Western Front.* New York: Fertig, 1996.

Kagan, Robert. "The Price of Hegemony: Can America Learn to Use Its Power?" *Foreign Affairs,* May/June 2022. https://www.foreignaffairs.com/articles/ukraine/2022-04-06/russia-ukraine-war-price-hegemony.

LeShan, Lawrence. *The Psychology of War.* New York: Helios, 1992.

Levi, Primo. *The Drowned and the Saved.* New York: Vintage, 1989.

———. *Survival in Auschwitz.* New York: Collier, 1987.

Mahedy, William P. *Out of the Night: The Spiritual Journey of Vietnam Vets.* New York: Ballantine Books, 1986.

Marbaker, Thomas D. *History of the Eleventh New Jersey Volunteers: From Its Organization to Appomattox.* Trenton: MacCrellish & Guigley, Book and Joe Printers, 1898.

Mearsheimer, John. *Liddell Hart and the Weight of History,* Ithaca: Cornell University Press, 2010.

Melman, Seymour. *Pentagon Capitalism: The Political Economy of War.* New York: McGraw-Hill Book Company, 1970.

Orwell, George. *Nineteen Eight-Four.* New York: Penguin Classics, 2021.

Sacco, Joe. *The Great War July 1, 1916: The First Day of the Battle of the Somme.* New York: W. W. Norton & Company, 2013.

Sereny, Gita. *Into That Darkness: An Examination of Conscience.* New York: Vintage Books, 1974.

Shapiro, Harold Roland. *What Every Young Man Should Know About War.* New York: Knight Publishers, 1937.

Shelley, Mary. *Frankenstein.* New York: Penguin Classics, 2018.

Sledge, E. B. *With the Old Breed: At Peleliu and Okinawa.* Oxford: Oxford University Press, 1981.

Smith, Mark. *The Smell of Battle, the Taste of Siege: A Sensory History of the Civil War.* New York: Oxford University Press, 2014.

Theweleit, Klaus. *Male Fantasies: Volumes 1 and 2.* Minneapolis: University of Minnesota Press, 1989.

Thompson, Mark. *A Paper House.* London: Vintage, 1992.

Trumbo, Dalton. *Johnny Got His Gun.* New York: Bantom, 1989.

Turner, Brian. *Here, Bullet.* Farmington, ME: Alice James Books, 2005.

Turse, Nick. *Kill Anything That Moves: The Real American War in Vietnam.* New York: Metropolitan Books, 2013.

van Agtmael, Peter. *2nd Tour Hope I Don't Die*. Photolucida, 2009.

Wikileaks. Classified Diplomatic Cable 08MOSCOW265_a. https://wikileaks.org/plusd/cables/08MOSCOW265_a.html.

Wolff, Leon. *In Flanders Fields: The 1917 Campaign*. London: The Folio Society, 2003.

NOTES

1. Vasily Grossman, *Everything Flows* (New York: New York Review of Books, 2009), 202.
2. E. B. Sledge, *With the Old Breed: At Peleliu and Okinawa* (Oxford: Oxford University Press, 1981), 100.
3. Ibid., 198–199.
4. Ibid., 147.
5. Barbara Foley, "Fact, Fiction, Fascism: Testimony and Mimesis in Holocaust Narratives," *Comparative Literature* XXXIV (Fall 1982), 333.
6. Ian Beacock, "The Democracy Walt Whitman Wanted," *The New Republic*, October 26, 2021.
7. W. H. Auden, "Epitaph on a Tyrant," *Selected Poems* (London: Faber and Faber, 1981), 80.
8. Wikileaks, Classified Diplomatic Cable 08MOSCOW265_a, https:// wikileaks.org/plusd/cables/08MOSCOW265_a.html.
9. Gabriel García Márquez, *Chronicle of a Death Foretold* (New York: Alfred A. Knopf, 1983), 50.
10. Cited in Raymond Bonner, "The Diplomat and the Killer," *The Atlantic*, February 11, 2016, https://www.theatlantic.com/international/archive/2016/02/el-salvador-churchwomen-murders/460320/.
11. Edward S. Herman and Noam Chomsky, *Manufacturing Consent: The Political Economy of the Mass Media* (New York: Pantheon Books, 1988), 32.
12. Nick Turse, *Kill Anything That Moves: The Real American War in Vietnam* (New York: Metropolitan Books, 2013), 79.
13. Ibid., 91.
14. Ibid., 224–225.
15. Ibid., 226.
16. Robert Kagan, "The Price of Hegemony: Can America Learn to Use Its Power?" *Foreign Affairs*, May/June 2022, https://www.foreignaffairs.com/articles/ukraine/2022-04-06/russia-ukraine-war-price-hegemony.
17. Kiš, Danilo, "On Nationalism," in the Appendix to Mark Thompson's *A Paper House* (London: Vintage, 1992), 339.
18. Elliott Abrams, "The New Cold War," *Council on Foreign Relations*, March 4, 2022, https://www.cfr.org/blog/new-cold-war-0.
19. Paul Fussell, *Wartime: Understanding and Behavior in the Second World War* (New York: Oxford University Press, 1989), 268.

20. Charles Krauthammer, "Victory Changes Everything . . . ," *Washington Post*, November 30, 2001.
21. "Testimony of William Kristol," Senate Foreign Relations Committee, February 7, 2002, https://avalon.law.yale.edu/sept11/kristol.asp.
22. Frederick W. Kagan, "The Decline of America's Armed Forces," in *Present Dangers: Crisis and Opportunity in American Foreign and Defense Policy*, eds. Robert Kagan and William Kristol (San Francisco: Encounter Books, 2000), 261.
23. Robert Kagan, "The Price of Hegemony: Can America Learn to Use Its Power?" *Foreign Affairs*, May/June 2022. https://www.foreignaffairs.com/articles/ukraine/2022-04-06/russia-ukraine-war-price-hegemony.
24. Brian Turner, *Here, Bullet* (Farmington, ME: Alice James Books, 2005), 18.
25. William P. Mahedy, *Out of the Night: The Spiritual Journey of Vietnam Vets* (New York: Ballantine Books, 1986), 7.
26. Ibid., 7.
27. Ibid., 115.
28. Chris Hedges and Laila Al-Arian, *Collateral Damage: America's War against Iraqi Civilians* (New York: Nation Books, 2008), xiv.
29. Ibid., xv–xvi.
30. Ibid., xvi.
31. Ibid., xix–xx.
32. Ibid., xxii.
33. Ibid., xxiii.
34. Ibid., xxvi.
35. Ibid. xxiii–xxiv.
36. Ibid., xxiv.
37. Ibid., xxvi.
38. Ibid., xxvi.
39. Ibid., xxvii.
40. Ibid., xxvii.
41. Klaus Theweleit, *Male Fantasies: Volume 2* (Minneapolis: University of Minnesota Press, 1989), 8.
42. Thomas Friedman, interview by Charlie Rose, *Charlie Rose*, May 30, 2003. https://charlierose.com/episodes/26893.
43. Theodor Adorno, *Critical Models: Interventions and Catchwords* (New York: Columbia University Press, 2005), 201.
44. Jess Goodell with John Hearn, *Shade It Black: Death and After in Iraq* (Havertown, PA: Casemate Publishers, 2011), 108–109.
45. Ibid., 119–120.
46. Dalton Trumbo, *Johnny Got His Gun* (New York: Bantam, 1989), 240–241.
47. Peter van Agtmael, *2nd Tour Hope I Don't Die* (Photolucida, 2009), 88.
48. Lori Grinker, *Afterwar: Veterans from a World of Conflict* (de.mo design limited, 2005), 58–59.
49. Ibid., 62–63.
50. Ibid., 96–97.
51. Ibid., 120–121.

52. Ibid., 124–125.
53. Timothy Findley, *Inside Memory: Pages from a Writer's Workbook* (Toronto: HarperCollins Publishers Ltd., 1990), 51.
54. Leon Wolff, *In Flanders Fields: The 1917 Campaign*, (London: The Folio Society, 2003), 108–109.
55. https://poetrytreasures.wordpress.com/2015/07/28/jack-fell-as-hed-have-wished-the-mother-said/.
56. Leon Wolff, *In Flanders Fields: The 1917 Campaign*, (London: The Folio Society, 2003), 253.
57. Cited in Jon Silkin, *Out of Battle: The Poetry of the Great War* (London: Palgrave Macmillan, 1998), 52.
58. Philip Gibbs, *Now It Can Be Told* (New York: Harper & Brothers, 1920), 143.
59. David Grossman, *On Killing: The Psychological Cost of Learning to Kill in War and Society* (Boston: Little, Brown, 1996), 43–44.
60. John Mearsheimer, *Liddell Hart and the Weight of History* (Ithaca: Cornell University Press, 2010), 60.
61. Harold Roland Shapiro, preface to *What Every Young Man Should Know About War* (New York: Knight Publishers, 1937).
62. Ibid., 20–21.
63. Franklin D. Jones, "Neuropsychiatric Casualties of Nuclear, Biological, and Chemical Warfare," in *Textbook of Military Medicine*, eds. Franklin D. Jones et al. (Falls Church, VA: Office of the Army Surgeon General, U.S. Army, 1995), 105.
64. Ernst Friedrich, *War against War* (Seattle, WA: The Real Comet Press, 1987), 109.
65. J. Glenn Gray, *The Warriors: Reflections on Men in Battle* (Lincoln: University of Nebraska Press, 1998), 21.
66. Primo Levi, *The Drowned and the Saved* (New York: Vintage, 1989), 31.
67. Ibid., 36.
68. Ibid., 69.
69. Allen C. Guelzo, *Gettysburg: The Last Invasion* (New York: Vintage Books, 2013), 35.
70. Ibid., 9.
71. Thomas D. Marbaker, *History of the Eleventh New Jersey Volunteers: From Its Organization to Appomattox* (Trenton: MacCrellish & Guigley, Book and Joe Printsers, 1898), 109.
72. Mark M. Smith, *The Smell of Battle, the Taste of Siege: A Sensory History of the Civil War* (New York: Oxford University Press, 2014), 167.
73. Allen C. Guelzo, *Gettysburg: The Last Invasion* (New York: Vintage Books, 2013), 275.
74. O. B. Curtis, *History of the 24th Michigan of Iron Brigade* (Detroit: Winn & Hammond, 1891), 144.
75. Ibid., 146.
76. Shelby Foote, *Stars in Their Courses: The Gettysburg Campaign, June–July 1863* (New York: The Modern Library, 1994), 86.

77. Randolph Bourne, *War and the Intellectuals* (Indianapolis: Hackett Publishing Company, Inc., 1999), 69.
78. Ibid., 67.
79. Fyodor Dostoevsky, *Notes from Underground* (New York: Alfred A. Knopf, 1993), 7.
80. Cited in Andrew J. Bacevich, *The Limits of Power: The End of American Exceptionalism* (New York: Metropolitan Books, 2008), 28–29.
81. Andrew J. Bacevich, *The Limits of Power: The End of American Exceptionalism* (New York: Metropolitan Books, 2008), 115.
82. Edward Gibbon, *The Decline and Fall of the Roman Empire*, vol. II (New York: Modern Library), 438.
83. Sigmund Freud, *Civilization and Its Discontents* (New York: W. W. Norton and Company, 1961), 81.
84. Ibid., 81.
85. Cited in Kai Bird and Martin J. Sherwin, *American Prometheus: The Triumph and Tragedy of J. Robert Oppenheimer* (New York: Vintage Books, 2005), 309.
86. James Baldwin, "Stranger in the Village," in *The Collected Essays of James Baldwin* (New York: The Library of America, 1998), 129.

INDEX

CHRIS HEDGES was a war correspondent for twenty years in Central America, the Middle East, Africa, and the Balkans, fifteen of them with the *New York Times,* where he was awarded the Pulitzer Prize. He is the author of fourteen books, including *War Is a Force That Gives Us Meaning, What Every Person Should Know about War, Collateral Damage: America's War against Iraqi Civilians,* which he co-authored with Laila Al-Arian, and *Our Class: Trauma and Transformation in an American Prison.* Passages in this book are taken from his writings on war, primarily from Truthdig and ScheerPost, over the past twenty years, as well as from numerous talks and lectures. It also draws on hundreds of hours of interviews with fifty combat veterans carried out for *Collateral Damage: America's War against Iraqi Civilians.* He writes a column every Monday for ScheerPost and has a show, the *Chris Hedges Report,* on the Real News Network. He holds a B.A. in English Literature from Colgate University and a Master of Divinity from Harvard University. He also studied Classics at Harvard University as a Nieman Fellow. He has taught at Columbia University, New York University, Princeton University, and the University of Toronto. He has taught students earning their college degree from Rutgers University in the New Jersey prison system since 2013. You can find him at chrishedges.substack.com.